# TEACH READING

## with **Orton-Gillingham**

*72* **Classroom-Ready Lessons** *to Help Struggling Readers and Students with Dyslexia Learn to* **Love Reading**

**Heather MacLeod-Vidal
& Kristina Smith**

 ULYSSES PRESS

Published in the US by:
ULYSSES PRESS
PO Box 3440
Berkeley, CA 94703
www.ulyssespress.com

ISBN: 978-1-64604-101-5
Library of Congress Control Number: 2020936430

Printed in the United States
10 9 8 7 6 5 4 3 2

Acquisitions editor: Casie Vogel
Managing editor: Claire Chun
Editor: Debra Riegert
Proofreader: Renee Rutledge
Front cover design: Justin Shirley
Cover art: © Lorelyn Medina/shutterstock.com
Interior design: what!design @ whatweb.com
Layout: Jake Flaherty

# CONTENTS

# INTRODUCTION

Dear Educator,

We created this fun and easy-to-follow Orton-Gillingham–based text with the goal of helping your students improve their literacy and learn to enjoy reading and writing. As former classroom teachers, we saw the need for a phonics-based curriculum that met the needs of our students with dyslexia and other learning differences. We both experienced situations with our students (ranging in age from pre-K through 6th grade) that were difficult to remedy with the typical reading and writing workshops available through our schools.

We became trained in the Orton-Gillingham approach and began utilizing the approach with our students in small groups and private tutoring sessions after school. After seeing the results, we set out to make a bigger impact on students with dyslexia. Heather Vidal started a local tutoring business, Treetops Educational Interventions, and Kristina Smith began working for Treetops shortly after it opened. We both left teaching full-time and began working with students in a one-on-one setting using an Orton-Gillingham approach that is easy to follow and does not require weeks of training.

From our experiences in the classroom, trainings, research, and thousands of private tutoring sessions, we have crafted this 72-lesson teacher's resource guide. Each lesson is designed to explicitly teach a phonetic skill, and each lesson thereafter builds upon the skills of previous lessons so your students will be constantly using and reviewing all they have learned.

Before diving in, it's important to recognize that this book is for students who struggle with literacy, including reading fluency, phonics, and spelling. In the next few pages, we will provide a brief overview of what dyslexia is, how it's diagnosed, and the effective teaching methods for working with those who are diagnosed. It is important to note that while this is a resource designed for students with dyslexia, this method of teaching has proven effective for many children who struggle with phonics and fluency. Again, teachers who have students that struggle with reading, especially those new to reading, will find that this resource provides a foundation and reinforces already-learned phonetic concepts to help create fluent readers.

Sincerely,

Heather and Kristina

# What Is Dyslexia?

People often think that dyslexia is strictly the confusion of similarly written letters, such as *b* and *d*, but it really encompasses much more. Dyslexia is a learning disorder that impacts one's ability to not only read, but to speak, spell, and write. Specifically, people with dyslexia may have difficulty with decoding, or identifying speech sounds, and learning how they relate to letters and words.[1] These difficulties typically result from a deficit in the phonological component of language. This, in turn, can lead to problems in reading comprehension and reduced reading experience that can impede growth of vocabulary and background knowledge.[2] These deficits have no impact on one's overall intelligence, for those with dyslexia often tend to be very fast and creative thinkers.[3] Typically, dyslexia is apparent in reading and language arts courses; however, students can struggle in any subject that contains any degree of reading. For example, they can have trouble reading and understanding math word problems. Dyslexia is considered to be the most common learning disability, affecting an estimated 17 percent of the population.[4] Of those who have a learning disability, dyslexia is found in 80 to 90 percent of the cases.[3] With prevalence rates this high, there is a very good chance that one of your students may be impacted by some degree of dyslexia.

## Signs of Dyslexia[5]

Noted below are some signs of dyslexia to watch for at various school ages.

### Preschool

- Late talking
- Learning new words slowly
- Trouble learning nursery rhymes or playing games that require recognizing rhyming patterns like hot, cot, and pot
- Difficulty learning the names of letters and letter sounds
- Problems forming words correctly—student may reverse sounds in words or confuse words that sound alike

## Elementary School

- Shows difficulty understanding and processing what they hear
- Demonstrates difficulty remembering the sequence of things
- Reads below grade level
- Labors over sounding out simple words, like dog or cat, and/or cannot sound out or pronounce an unfamiliar word
- Struggles with coming up with the right word or forming the right answer to a question
- Labors over seeing (and occasionally hearing) similarities and differences in letter sounds and words (such as rhyming words or ones that begin with the same letter)
- Struggles with spelling; may not associate letters with sounds, like the letter *f* with the /f/ sound, as in fox
- Takes an unusually long time reading or writing, slowly acquires reading skill, or avoids activities that involve reading altogether

# Diagnosing Dyslexia[6]

No single test can diagnose dyslexia, and a lot of factors may impact your student's ability to read that may not include dyslexia. The Mayo Clinic suggests the use of one or more of the tools listed below to help determine if a child is dyslexic. Only a professional can accurately diagnose your student.

- Vision, hearing, and brain (neurological) tests to help rule out any other potential disorders affecting your student's reading ability.
- A home life assessment to ensure the home setting is conducive to a proper learning environment.
- A developmental and medical history to assess the student's physical history and whether or not any medical conditions or learning disabilities related to the student's education may run in the family.
- Psychological testing to assess the student's mental health and to help determine if any mental health issues are contributing to the student's struggle with reading. Issues like depression and anxiety can play a significant role.
- Questionnaires taken by the student, family, and teacher to help pinpoint specific difficulties the student is struggling with.
- Reading assessments with the results analyzed by a reading expert.

---

6   "Dyslexia," Mayo Clinic, last modified July 22, 2017, https://www.mayoclinic.org/diseases-conditions/dyslexia/diagnosis-treatment/drc-20353557.

# Helping Students with Dyslexia

## Effective Methods for Teaching Students with Dyslexia

Early literacy studies suggest that high-quality instruction consists of core literacy skills that target multiple areas of instruction, such as phonological awareness and word, syllable, and phonemic levels.[7] The most significant characteristic of high-quality intervention is that there is an explicit approach to teaching the sounds of letters in isolation, which are then blended to form words.[7] For example, an explicit approach to teaching spends multiple lessons reviewing the individual sounds for the letters *d, o, g,* and then in future lessons, demonstrates the blending of those letter sounds to form the word dog. This method helps the struggling reader decode words and then apply the same method to future and unfamiliar words.

Some methods of teaching literacy involve an implicit approach in which the instruction focuses on the identification of letter sounds within the context of the whole word.[7] For example, showing the word dog along with a picture of a dog to serve as a clue to the word. While this method is effective for some, it is not the most beneficial for struggling readers.

Dyslexia can't be cured, but with the right support and instruction, reading can be made easier—and fun! *Teach Reading with Orton-Gillingham* is based on the aforementioned explicit approach to teaching using the Orton-Gillingham (OG) method to create a multisensory model of instruction.

## Brief History of Orton-Gillingham

The principles of Orton-Gillingham were established by Samuel T. Orton, a neuropsychiatrist and pathologist, and Anna Gillingham, an educator and psychologist, in the 1930s and 1940s.[8]

---

7   E. J. Daly, S. Neugebauer, S. Chafouleas, and C. H. Skinner, *Interventions for Reading Problems: Designing and Evaluating Effective Strategies*, 2nd ed., (New York: Guilford Publications, 2015).

8   K. L. Sayeski, G. A. Earle, R. Davis, and J. Calamari, "Orton Gillingham: Who, What, and How," *TEACHING Exceptional Children* 51, no. 3 (December 2018): 240–249, doi: 10.1177/0040059918816996.

They created an approach to reading that (a) explicitly taught students the elements of language such as phonology, syllabification, and morphology, and (b) facilitated students' automaticity in applying this knowledge to the decoding (reading) and encoding (spelling) of language.

# The Orton-Gillingham Approach to Teaching

Essentially, the OG approach to reading instruction is based on breaking down language into individual and overlapping skills. The educator then creates instructional activities designed to promote mastery and automaticity of those skills.[8]

Sayeski et al. state several distinguishing features of the OG teaching approach:

1. Direct, systematic, incremental, and cumulative lessons, including oral reading, spelling, and new concept instruction.
2. Cognitive explanations, such as teaching phonics rules.
3. Diagnostic and prescriptive methods, such as planning lessons based on how the student performs in the current lesson.
4. Linguistics-based instruction, such as lessons that address topics like word families, blending, and handwriting.
5. Multisensory engagement, such as teaching and repeating a letter sound, visualizing and writing the letter, and forming the letter with a tactile material such as dough.

# Why Use This Book

Research shows that the explicit approach to teaching literacy is the most effective technique to use with struggling readers. The Orton-Gillingham method combines that approach along with a multisensory model to teach and reinforce literacy skills. Using OG as its foundation, *Teach Reading with Orton-Gillingham* contains lessons, activities, and assessments to provide teachers with a clear and easy-to-use resource to improve their students' literacy while making it fun!

# How to Use This Book

## Getting Started

### Necessary Materials

This book includes the foundation necessary to get started with an Orton-Gillingham approach. In order to make the lessons multisensory, it is helpful to have the following materials:

- Pencils
- Index cards
- "Bumpy" board (a plastic weaving sheet that can be purchased at a craft store)
- Plastic tray for tactile writing
- Tactile material for the tray, such as sand, shaving cream, or plastic water beads
- Counters, such as pennies, to model sounds

### Supplemental Materials

These materials are not necessary, but our students love them:

- Supplemental worksheets found at www.treetopseducation.com
- Buddha Board (a water-painting board)
- Magnetic doodle board
- Sidewalk chalk
- Letter magnets
- Play-Doh
- Pointer or fly swatter
- Surfaces with interesting textures, such as sandpaper, carpet squares, or fabric

## Notebook Organization

In order to stay organized, it is important for students to keep a notebook dedicated to their work in the Orton-Gillingham system. A composition notebook divided into the following sections is best:

1. Notes
2. Spelling Rules
3. Assessment
4. Sight Words

*Suggested notebook*

## Suggested Lesson Breakdown

We recommend taking at least a week or three sessions for each lesson. Some lessons may take longer based on their complexity. Here is our suggested time breakdown based on three 30-minute lessons per week.

**Day 1**
- Review previous concept(s)
- Introduce new concept
  - Mouth movement (Unit 1)
  - Letter formation (Unit 1)
  - Elkonin boxes
  - Syllabication (Units 3–9)
  - Teacher modeling

**Day 2**
- Review previous concept(s), review current concept
- Concept-Picture Connection (index cards). See page 14 for an example.
- Multisensory Connection

**Day 3**
- Review previous concept(s), review current concept
- Sight Word practice
- Decodable reading
- Assessment (if applicable)

## Comprehension

Orton-Gillingham is a phonics program, but it is essential that reading lessons include comprehension instruction as well. We recommend 30 minutes of phonics instruction with an additional 15–30 minutes of comprehension instruction. Phonics is essential to improving students' fluency (and therefore enjoyment of reading). It is likely that reading comprehension will improve with time using this program.[9] Reading comprehension can be taught through

---

9   V. Connelly, R. S. Johnston, and G. B. Thompson, "The Effects of Phonics Instruction on the Reading Comprehension of Beginning Readers," *Reading and Writing* 14, no. 5 (September 2001): 423–457, doi: 10.1023/A:1011114724881.

read-alouds, book clubs, and guided reading. Research has shown that reading instruction is most effective when utilizing authentic novels, stories, and articles as opposed to textbooks. To make your comprehension lesson as effective as possible, include instruction on comprehension skills within a variety of texts. Be sure to utilize a variety of genres, including poetry, fantasy, and nonfiction.

Be sure to include instruction in one of these skills in each reading lesson:

- Making connections
- Visualizing
- Retelling
- Wondering
- Making inferences
- Determining important ideas
- Text features
- Text structure
- Author's purpose
- Synthesizing information across multiple sources

# Review

Review is a crucial part of any Orton-Gillingham lesson. Students with dyslexia and other reading differences depend on the explicit nature of the Orton-Gillingham approach. A consistent routine with a review at its forefront helps students build the necessary phonetic skills needed in order to build connections.

We recommend devoting 10 minutes at the beginning of each lesson to review previous concepts, spelling rules, and sight words. A multisensory review is preferred. These are the activities and methods that we recommend using.

### THE DOS AND DON'TS OF REVIEW

| Do | Don't |
|---|---|
| • Switch up your review activities often.<br>• Review both concepts and sight words.<br>• Keep it fun and brief.<br>• Rotate between concepts that you know your student(s) are strong in and ones that they need more work on.<br>• Use the information you glean from review as an informal assessment.<br>• Keep notes on concepts your student(s) miss during the review. If you notice a pattern of struggle, go back and reteach the lesson(s). | • Don't use the same activity every time.<br>• Don't stick to reviewing just the previous lesson. You should be revisiting all concepts that your student has trouble with (even things that they have previously mastered).<br>• Don't rely on pen and paper review activities. Multisensory instruction is a crucial part of the review, and of the Orton-Gillingham approach as a whole. |

Orton-Gillingham is often used as an individualized approach, but many teachers implement these strategies with a group. Many of the ideas in this text can be modified for use in an individual or group setting.

## Ideas for Review

**List It!:** Students turn and talk or independently come up with as many words as possible that showcase a previous skill. They can list these in a notebook, complete the exercise orally, or take turns listing them on the board in a word relay.

**Identify It!:** Show students a few pictures and ask which ones start with or contain the letter pattern that you request. To make it more fun, have students use pointers or fly swatters to smack the words.

**Mold It!:** Use a material like clay, Play-Doh, or wax sticks to mold letters and words.

**Assess It!:** Give students a mini spelling assessment. This should only be used after several skills have been covered.

**Painting:** Have students practice letter writing through painting. This can involve finger painting, painting with a brush, or even using a canvas board with water, such as a Buddha Board.

*Listing and molding words to review a previous skill.*

**Tactile Reinforcement:** Using a tactile material (sand, small beads, shaving cream, hair gel, sandpaper, rug squares, etc.), call out sounds or words for students to write. Circulate while they work, and always demonstrate the correct sound to ensure that students are able to self-correct as needed.

**Hopscotch:** Write previous skills in hopscotch squares. Have students hop from concept to concept while making the associated sounds. We also use this for sight words.

*Tactile reinforcement of sounds.*

**Red Light, Green Light:** Hold up the index cards made during each lesson. Instruct students to name the letter, associated picture, and the letter's sound (for the card *p*, they would say, *p*, pig, and then make the /p/ sound). If they get it correct, they can take a jump forward. If they get it wrong, they stay in place. The goal is to reach the instructor by jumping forward with each correct answer.

# Introduction of a New Concept

When introducing a new concept, it is necessary to provide explicit, direct instruction. Oftentimes, lessons must be broken down into small, manageable parts. The Orton-Gillingham approach demands that students are taught to encode (write and spell) words prior to learning to decode (read).

Specific tips are presented before each unit in this book, and all lessons include letter-sound connections and teacher-modeling ideas.

# Mouth Movement

Unit 1: Consonants, Consonant Digraphs, and Short Vowels, includes specific instructions for mouth movement. The explicit nature of teaching mouth movements is helpful for young children who are having difficulty connecting graphemes (letters) to sounds. The mouth chart can be used to offer students a visual representation as to how their mouth should look when articulating each letter sound. If you would like more detailed instruction on the proper mouth movements, please visit our website: www.treetopseducation.com.

# Letter Formation

It is vital to establish proper habits for handwriting. The correct print formation will carry over into cursive.

Experiment with different size letters to determine if the student has an easier time with larger or smaller sizes. This information can be used to drive instruction and help students achieve success.

# Multisensory Activities to Improve Handwriting

- Use a wet sponge to write the letter on the pavement.
- Practice "sky-writing" by writing the letter in the air.
- Use a wet paintbrush to form the letter either in the air or on a surface.

*Using a wet paintbrush (top) and Play-Doh (bottom) as a tool to improve handwriting.*

- Give students Play-Doh rolled into snakes. Ask them to lay down the Play-Doh into the correct letter formation using the same directional cues they would use to write the letter. After students form the letter, have them trace it with their finger using correct directional cues.
- Trace the letter using their index finger on a tactile material, such as sandpaper, a plastic weaving board, or a carpet square.

# Teacher Modeling

When modeling a new concept, teachers must use several methodologies. Visual representations paired with auditory instruction help students with a variety of learning preferences. In this section, teachers model tapping, building words, and blending words. During this segment of the lesson, we recommend teaching students to copy down the words used to start the lesson. This is typically a list of four to eight words. This list should be written in the Notes section of their OG notebooks. When teaching a spelling rule, ask the students to copy the rule(s) in the Spelling Rules portion of their notebook.

# Finger Tapping

Finger tapping is a must when using the Orton-Gillingham method. Tapping helps build the idea that sounds and graphemes are connected. This multisensory method is easy to implement and essential within the OG approach.

Students need to understand that letters have their own sounds, but they slide into the next sound without pause. Teach students to tap on the hand they do not write with so they can practice tapping as they write.

To be clear, finger tapping is more about associating sounds with letters, so tapping will not include silent letters. For words with more than five sounds, students can start again from their first finger.

Finger-Tapping Rules:

1. Tap once for each sound.
2. Digraphs get one tap only (*th*, *sh*, *wh*, *ch*, etc.).
3. Vowel teams get one tap only (*ea*, *ee*, *oa*, *ai*, *igh*, etc.).
4. Glued sounds are tapped once with as many fingers as there are letters in the sound (for example, *-ild* is tapped once with three fingers together).
5. Silent letters are not tapped, just sounds that are heard.

# Elkonin Boxes

Elkonin boxes are a useful way to connect correct spelling with finger tapping. The boxes teach students to segment words into their phonological parts. Each box represents a sound, but boxes can contain more than one letter if a consonant digraph, vowel team, or glued sound is in the word. Specific examples of Elkonin boxes are used in some lessons, and the Tips, Tricks, and Things to Know section at the start of each unit shows more specific details about using Elkonin boxes within said skill(s). When creating Elkonin boxes for students, many teachers choose to design the boxes in a way that gives the student a hint about the length of the word, the height of letters, etc.

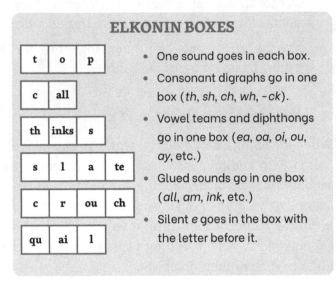

**ELKONIN BOXES**

| t | o | p | |
|---|---|---|---|

| c | all | |
|---|---|---|

| th | inks | s |
|---|---|---|

| s | l | a | te |
|---|---|---|---|

| c | r | ou | ch |
|---|---|---|---|

| qu | ai | l |
|---|---|---|

- One sound goes in each box.
- Consonant digraphs go in one box (*th*, *sh*, *ch*, *wh*, *-ck*).
- Vowel teams and diphthongs go in one box (*ea*, *oa*, *oi*, *ou*, *ay*, etc.)
- Glued sounds go in one box (*all*, *am*, *ink*, etc.)
- Silent *e* goes in the box with the letter before it.

# Syllabication

We begin teaching syllabication in Unit 3: Closed Syllables. Each unit includes specific tips for syllabication; however, there are some important rules and patterns to know prior to starting instruction on how to break words into syllables.

## TYPES OF SYLLABLES*

| | Single Syllable | Multisyllabic |
|---|---|---|
| **Closed** | pan, snack, shrimp | **cat**/nip, **in**/dex, **rab**/bit |
| **Silent *e*** | cake, time, stone | pine/**cone**, sun/**shine** |
| **Vowel Team/Diphthong** | beach, boat, tree, trout, spoil, taught | **rai**/sin, **pea**/nut, with/**out**, **Au**/gust |
| **Open** | why, be | **bo**/nus, **mu**/sic, **ba**/by |
| ***r*-influenced** | fern, hurt, bird | spi/**der**, **twirl**/ing |
| **Consonant -*le*** | None | a/**ble**, trem/**ble** |

*Bolded letters model the taught skill.*

**Rules**

1. All syllables have one vowel sound.
2. Compound words should be divided between the two base words.
3. If two consonants appear in between two vowels, divide them in half.
4. If three consonants appear between two vowels, determine which two belong together. Blends and digraphs should not be separated.
5. When one consonant is in-between two vowels, first try dividing after the consonant to keep the vowel "closed in." If that doesn't sound right, try dividing before the consonant to keep the vowel open.
6. Never divide a vowel team or diphthong in half.
7. If there are two vowels in the middle of a multisyllabic word that do not work as a team, divide them in half.
8. The syllable type consonant -*le* pattern is its own syllable and should be divided as one.

## Syllabication Activity Ideas

**Ideas with Index Cards**

- Use Play-Doh to "scoop" syllables.
- Have students cut syllables in half. Then play concentration with the separated pieces.
- Use straws to separate syllables.

**Ideas with Movement**

- Teach students to "pound" out syllables with their fists on a table. This can be combined with finger tapping to practice both spelling and breaking words into syllables.
- Play Head, Shoulders, Knees, and Toes. Have students start by touching their head then working downward (and back up if needed) to tap each syllable out.
- March out syllables by having students march in place and jump after the entire word.

*Syllabication ideas with index cards*

# Concept-Picture Connection

During this segment of the lesson, students review previous index cards and create new index cards as seen in the example to the right. The cards include the letter along with its associated "guide word." This guide word is used in the introduction of the concept. Go to page 286 for a complete list of guide words. To review previous cards, hold the cards facing your student as you would a flashcard. Tell your students to say the letter on the card, followed by the guide word, followed by the sound. For example, for the letter *p*, the student will say, *p*, pig, /p/. It is not necessary to review every card every time, especially if your student has mastered the skill with nearly 100 percent accuracy; however, you must review any new or tricky concepts on a regular basis. To keep your cards organized, we recommend keeping them on a ring.

# Multisensory Connections

The Orton-Gillingham approach works because it solidifies concepts for students via multisensory connections. While it is sometimes tempting to skip these messy" materials, they are truly essential to building those connections among students who struggle with reading. This is the point in the lesson in which students begin to apply the spelling concept to more independent tasks. The teacher reads a word or a segment of a word from an earlier lesson. The student then writes the word using a tactile material, such as sand, shaving cream, water beads, or hair gel. We recommend changing materials often to keep this part of the lesson fun and engaging.

For example, the teacher will say, "blot," the students should then say, "blot," begin writing and spelling out loud at the same time "b-l-o-t," and then repeat "blot" after spelling. If there are more than a few students, whispering may be preferred. This should be modeled many times as a procedure.

Use the list of words provided in each lesson to guide instruction. Depending on the students' needs, you may need to dictate each sound in the word.

When you begin teaching syllabication, it is helpful to have students write the word on a tactile tray and then put a slash between the syllables.

# Words with Multiple Spelling Options

As students get further into the program, they will begin to notice that there are many spelling patterns that make the same sound. For example, the long *a* pattern can be represented with a silent *e, ai, ay,* and *eigh.* It is important to acknowledge how positive it is that the student remembers the different patterns. At the same time, it is important to correct misspellings when they happen and point out any clues that might help students determine which pattern is the most likely in a selected word. Oftentimes, there are specific instances that dictate when to use each pattern, but when there is not, teach students to try the most likely option first, followed by the next most likely option if the first is not correct. For example, when teaching the *r*-influenced vowel sounds *er, ir,* and *ur,* it is helpful for students to know that *er* is the most common pattern, followed by *ur* and then *ir.* Tips like these are included in each unit's Tips, Tricks, and Things to Know section. These rules should be copied into the Spelling Rules portion of students' notebooks.

# Homophones, Homonyms, and Homographs

Observant students will begin to notice that there are many words with the same spelling, sound, or both! Orton-Gillingham instructors should teach the concept of homophones, homonyms, and homographs early in the program. To make this concept fun for students, keep a running homophone and homograph wall. When a student discovers a word that falls under one of these categories, they can create an index card with the alternate words.

| Homonyms | Homophones | Homographs |
|---|---|---|
| Words that are pronounced the same but may be spelled the same or differently. Their meanings are different. These refer to both homophones or homographs.<br><br>Examples:<br>• beet-beat<br>• bear-bare<br>• letter-letter | Words that are pronounced the same, but spelled differently. Their meanings are different.<br><br>Examples:<br>• pair-pear<br>• hear-here<br>• fare-fair | Words that are spelled the same but are pronounced differently and have different meanings.<br><br>Examples:<br>• bow(hair)-bow(ship)<br>• minute(tiny)-minute(time)<br>• rebel (noun)-rebel (verb) |

# Sight Words

Sight words are an important part of teaching reading. Sight words are high-frequency words, which are sometimes non-phonetic, that should be memorized. To be clear, there are very few words that do not follow the conventional rules of English. With that being said, students often do not possess the necessary reading skills early enough in their reading journey to read many high-frequency words. Because of this, it is essential to incorporate sight word instruction into your lessons. Students may realize later in their lessons that some of the words they learned as sight words are actually phonetic! If you are working within a classroom that has a word wall, you may choose to remove words from the word wall once they become phonetic.

There are suggested sight words in each lesson, but if your students have already mastered the suggested sight words, choose a word that you notice them misspelling in their writing. You may also reference the list of sight words in the Appendix on page 280.

## Procedure to Introduce New Sight Words

1. First, introduce the word by writing it in pencil on a blank index card. Write the word slowly to model correct letter formation. Place the index card in front of the students.

2. Now, model arm tapping.

   - Stand up and hold out your nondominant arm.

   - Say the selected sight word. For example, "very."

   - Using your dominant hand, start at the top of your arm to tap out the selected sight word. Tap one time for each letter as you spell out the word. For example, to tap out the sight word "very," tap four times starting from the shoulder and moving down to the wrist as you say "v-e-r-y." Using a singsong voice or rhythm helps students retain the word.

   - Once you finish tapping the word, slide your dominant hand from the shoulder to the wrist as you say the sight word again.

   - Have students follow this procedure three times, or until they can spell the word without looking at the index card.

3. Next, place the index card with the word written in pencil over a bumpy board.

4. Ask students to trace the word on an index card with a crayon. By tracing the word with a crayon over the bumpy board, the word will become bumpy, which is essential for the next step.

5. Tell students to use the index finger from their dominant hand to trace the word as they say the letters.

6. After completing the procedure for the week's sight words, place the sight words on a ring for easy practice. When your students are consistently reading and spelling the words correctly, you may choose to "retire the words from practice.

7. To complete the Sight Words portion of the lesson, tell students to write sentences using each of the week's sight words in the Sight Words section of their notebook.

**Important note: Students should never arm-tap sounds, only letters. It is important to differentiate arm tapping (letters) from finger tapping (sounds).**

## Additional Practice

If you notice that students are misspelling sight words that have already been covered, have them continue to practice using the words by writing the missed words in the Sight Words section of their OG notebook. You may choose to have them write the word three times each, use rainbow writing, or use word ladders to reinforce correct spelling.

# Decodable Reading

To truly teach and assess a student's progress using the Orton-Gillingham approach, it is essential that the passages they are expected to read include only the phonetic concepts and sight words that they have learned up to that point in the program. The words, sentences, and passages in this text include only the skills that students have learned, so they are an accurate representation of a student's proficiency. One may notice that while students are able to master the words and sentences in this text, they may still flounder on grade-level texts outside of the program. This is normal, especially within the first units of this book, since students have not yet mastered all of the skills necessary to experience success in a text that may include many more concepts. Rest assured that a clear carryover of skills will occur once students have mastered more phonetic patterns and concepts.

## Nonsense Words

Many of the lessons in this text include nonsense words. The purpose of teaching and assessing using nonsense words is to ensure that students have truly mastered the phonetic skills. In a 2016 study, researchers found that "forcing learners to attend to phonetic details during perceptual training resulted in significant improvement in pronunciation."[10] Students are required to connect the graphemes with phonemes rather than relying on memory alone. As previously stated, children with dyslexia are often exceptionally bright. Because of this, they have often memorized many words. This may make them appear to be proficient readers at first, but with a closer examination, teachers will discover that they do not possess knowledge of the common spelling patterns necessary to decode more challenging or unfamiliar words.

10   R. Thomson and T. Derwing, "Is Phonemic Training Using Nonsense or Real Words More Effective?" *Proceedings of the 7th Pronunciation in Second Language Learning and Teaching Conference* (2016): 88–97.

# Assessment

Assessments should be done in a one-on-one setting to determine a student's strengths and weaknesses. Directions should always be read to students to ensure they are only tested on the specific phonetic skills from the unit.

## Where to Start

This book includes an assessment (see the Appendix on page 280) to determine where to start your student. This assessment can also be used each year to confirm mastery of covered skills. The assessment includes sections to assess both reading and spelling and a sight word section to drive instruction.

## Unit Tests

Each unit includes a pretest and a post-test. Use these tests to assess progress and to determine if it is necessary to reteach any previous concepts. We also encourage you to conduct informal assessments during each lesson. This may mean marking down incorrect answers on the decodable reading section or identifying errors during multisensory practice. Each unit includes periodic mini assessments to assess progress and determine if your student is ready to move on. To keep track of assessment scores, you may choose to glue students' assessments into the Assessment portion of their notebooks.

## Moving On

A student is considered proficient and ready to move on if they can correctly read and spell 85 percent of the words within the lesson. Some lessons may take more time than others. Scaffold your instruction to the needs of your students.

## Additional Practice

This text includes a large list of words and sentences. With that being said, your students may require additional practice for some lessons. For more words, sentences, decodable stories, flip books, and games, visit our website: www.treetopseducation.com.

# Unit 1: Consonants, Consonant Digraphs, and Short Vowels

## Tips, Tricks, and Things to Know

In this unit, students learn how to read and spell words with consonants, consonant digraphs, and short vowels. Three spelling rules, *c* versus *k*, *-k*, *-ck*, or *-c*, the doubling rule, and the plural spelling rule, are also reviewed.

### Mouth Movements

This unit includes specific instructions for mouth movements to form letters. The explicit teaching of mouth movements is helpful for students who struggle with making the connection between letters and sounds. The chart below provides a visual for your students to reference; or, they can visit our website at www.treetopseducation.com for more detailed videos.

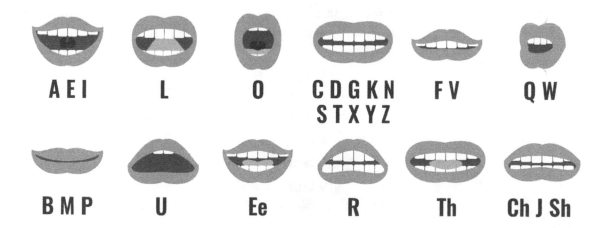

|  |  |  |  |  |  |
|---|---|---|---|---|---|
| A E I | L | O | C D G K N S T X Y Z | F V | Q W |
| B M P | U | Ee | R | Th | Ch J Sh |

To make the mouth movements and sounds more concrete, encourage students to practice while looking in a mirror or camera.

This chapter also introduces the concept of voiced and unvoiced letters. To make an unvoiced letter, you release air, while a voiced letter releases sound from the throat. Many of the letters in this lesson are taught as voiced and unvoiced pairs. This means that the letters are formed with the same mouth movement, but one is voiced and the other is unvoiced.

## Letter Sound Connections

Each lesson includes a list of letter sound connections. Students should listen to the list of words in each lesson. After each one, encourage them to give you a thumbs up or a thumbs down if they hear the sound of the letter you are practicing.

## Letter Formation

Encourage students to practice correct posture and grip to establish healthy handwriting habits. Some handwriting practice is provided, but if you need additional ideas, feel free to visit our website at www.treetopseducation.com.

## Multisensory Connections

In several of the lessons in this unit, students will be asked to only write the initial letter sound on the list of words using the day's multisensory material (see page 10 for ideas and more detailed instructions for using multisensory material). Once they learn vowel sounds, they will begin attempting to write full words, both real and nonsense.

## Finger Tapping

When finger tapping, each letter should be tapped so long as it makes its own sound. It is important to point out that consonant digraphs (*ck*, *ch*, *sh*, *th*, and *wh*) all make one sound. In addition, sounds such as *ss*, *ff*, *ll*, and *zz* are all one tap as well because they make one sound.

Here are some examples:

| | | |
|---|---|---|
| fig | 3 taps | f-i-g |
| luck | 3 taps | l-u-ck |
| mess | 3 taps | m-e-ss |
| cash | 3 taps | c-a-sh |
| it | 2 taps | i-t |

## Elkonin Boxes

The same finger-tapping rules above apply to Elkonin boxes. Here are a few examples.

| b | i | g |
|---|---|---|
| p | e | t |
| a | t |   |
| ch | i | p |
| d | u | ck |
| m | o | ss |

## Spelling Rules

**c/k:** Hard *c* is used before consonants and the vowels *a*, *o*, and *u*. *K* is used before *e* and *i*.

*Exceptions*: Words such as koala, kangaroo, Korea, skate, Kung Fu, and skull.

**k/-ck, -c:** *-ck* is used at the end of a one-syllable word right after a short vowel. Use *k* in all other instances. The ending *-c*, or more specifically *-ic*, goes at the end of a two-syllable word ending in the /k/ sound.

*Exceptions*: When a suffix begins with *e*, *i*, or *y*, add a *k* after the *c* as in mimic-mimicked or panic-panicking.

**The Doubling Rule:** If a word ends with a short vowel followed by *f*, *l*, *s*, or *z*, double it!

*Exceptions*: Words such as gross, bus, chef, and gal.

**Plural Spelling Rules:**

- If a word ends with *-sh*, *-ch*, *x*, *s*, *z*, or a consonant plus *o*, add *-es*.
- If a word ends in *f*, change it to *v* and add *-es*.
- For all other words, add *-s*.
- When a word ends in *s*, the *s* may sound like /s/ or /z/.

*Exceptions*: This rule does not apply to irregular nouns such as mouse-mice, tooth-teeth, foot-feet, man-men, fish, sheep, or deer.

## Guide Words

Below are the guide words used in the lesson. Guide words are a visual representation that highlight the taught skill. Use these words when referring to a specific skill. Do not make cards for the italicized words since their concepts are not fully covered until later units, but they are here for your reference.

By the end of the unit, students should have a total of 37 Concept-Word Connection Cards with these guide words.

1. *p*, *b*: pig, bat
2. *t*, *d*: tree, dinosaur
3. *k*, *g*: kit, grapes
4. Short *i*: igloo
5. *f*, *v*: flower, van
6. Short *e*: elephant
7. *s*, *z*: sun, zipper
8. Short *a*: alligator
9. *ch*, *j*: cheese, jam
10. *m*, *n*: monster, nest
11. Short *o*: olive
12. *w*, *h*, *wh*: wing, hive, whisper
13. *l*, *r*: list, railroad
14. Short *u*: umbrella

Spelling Rule *c*, *k*, -*ck*: cat, kit, duck

15. *x*: fox, xylophone, *exist*
16. *y*: yak
17. *qu*: question
18. Hard and soft *th*: thunder, there
19. *Sh* /zsh/: shell, measure

The Doubling Rule *ss*, *ll*, *ff*, *zz*: kiss

Plural Spelling Rule -*s*, -*es*, -*lves*: frogs, halves, wishes

## Sight Words

Here are the sight words covered in this unit:

| | | | | |
|---|---|---|---|---|
| and | we | *my* | like | on |
| the | by | to | *will* | make |
| be | a | she | see | down |
| look | no | he | them | how |
| said | at | was | in | or |
| you | but | one | *first* | with |
| can | get | two | come | may |
| go | all | did | not | then |
| I | of | when | have | than |
| so | is | which | this | out |
| do | day | had | it | more |

Name: _____     Date: _____

# Unit 1 Pretest

**Read the words below.**

|       |       |       |
|-------|-------|-------|
| pit   | quit  | mod   |
| sat   | miss  | led   |
| kid   | fizz  | cup   |
| with  | rock  | yet   |

**Read the sentences below.**

1. Look at the red cat and the big pig.
2. Which lock did she get?
3. Will you make the chips and dip?
4. I can see the duck, but I do not see the rat.

**Write the correct spelling for each picture.**

_____          _____

_____          _____

**Circle the pictures that rhyme.**

# Practice Literacy at Home

Dear Parents/Guardians,

We have begun our literacy journey into Unit 1: Consonants, Consonant Digraphs, and Short Vowels. Each lesson focuses on specific letter sounds and builds upon previous lessons to ensure retention. All of the vowels reviewed are short and the consonant digraphs (two consonants when put together that make one sound) taught in this unit are -*ck* (as in duck), *ch* (chat), *th* (that), *wh* (whip), and *sh* (fish). Two spelling rules will also be taught in this unit. The first is the doubling rule. It says that if a word ends with a short vowel followed by *f, l, s, or z*, double it. The second is a plural rule. This says that if a word ends with -*sh*, -*ch*, *x, s, z*, or a consonant plus *o*, add -*es*. If a word ends in *f*, change it to *v* and add -*es*. For all other words, add -*s*. By the end, your child should be able to recognize each letter's sound, as well as read and spell basic one-syllable short vowel words.

If you'd like your child to practice this unit at home, here are the prospective dates for each lesson and some words they can practice sound-identifying, reading, writing, and spelling. The goal of the first three lessons is to identify the specified letter sound in words. Reading and spelling begin after the short *i* lesson.

| Dates: | | | | | | | | | | | |
|---|---|---|---|---|---|---|---|---|---|---|---|
| Skills: | *p, b* | *t, d* | *k, g* | Short *i* | *f, v* | Short *e* | *s, z* | Short *a* | *ch, j* | *m, n* | Short *o* |
| Examples: | puck<br>bat<br>pop | tent<br>dip<br>dad | key<br>gap<br>king | kid<br>pig<br>bit | fit<br>vid<br>fig | bet<br>bed<br>get | set<br>zit<br>sip | gas<br>zag<br>vat | chip<br>jet<br>chat | mat<br>nap<br>mag | jot<br>dog<br>mom |

| Dates: | | | | | | | | | | | |
|---|---|---|---|---|---|---|---|---|---|---|---|
| Skills: | *w, h,*<br>*wh* | *l, r* | Short *u* | *c, k,*<br>–*ck* | *x* | *y* | *qu* | *th* | *sh* | Doubling<br>Rule | Plurals |
| Examples: | wig<br>hog<br>whip | lap<br>rat<br>red | mug<br>hug<br>bug | cup<br>kick<br>sock | fox<br>mix<br>six | yak<br>yap<br>yet | quiz<br>quit<br>quick | bath<br>then<br>path | ship<br>fish<br>shop | miss<br>doll<br>puff | cats<br>kisses<br>calves |

To make reading and writing even more fun, have your child use Play-Doh, colored markers, or pencils to spell each word. They can even pick some of the words to draw and label!

Happy learning!

# Lesson 1 | Consonants *p* & *b*

The first few lessons of this unit are a bit shorter since students will not start reading words until learning their first vowel in Lesson 4 on page 34.

## *Pretest*

## Introduce the New Concept

Today's lesson introduces students to their first two consonant sounds. Encourage them to listen to the initial sounds in the following words:

| *p* | *b* |
|---|---|
| pig | bat |
| pan | bug |
| pet | bend |

Explain that both of these letters have a special name, "lip poppers." This is because of the way your mouth moves when you make the letters' sounds.

To make a "lip popper," tell students to clasp their lips and then release a puff of air to make the unvoiced /p/ sound. To make a voiced /b/ sound, they should make the same mouth movement, but this time, instead of just releasing air, release the sound from their throats. To provide a clear example, have students put their hands on their throats so they can feel the movement when they make the /b/ sound. Then have them switch between making the /p/ and /b/ sound while still keeping a hand on their throat to feel the difference.

## Letter Sound Connections

Ask students to listen to the following list of words. After each one, encourage them to give you a thumbs up or a thumbs down if they hear the sound of the letter you are practicing.

| *b* | *p* |
|---|---|
| banana | possum |
| minute | juggle |
| ball | mouse |
| bull | pit |
| valley | puddle |

## Concept-Picture Connection

Students should draw a picture on an index card of the following guide words. See Guide Words on page 22 for more details.

Guide Word(s): pig, bat

## Multisensory Connections

Tell students to listen to the following sounds or the initial letter sounds in the words. Instruct them to write the letter in their tactile material. Please refer to page 10 for more detailed information.

| | | | |
|---|---|---|---|
| p | b | pot | bugs |
| b | p | banana | plan |

## Sight Words

Create index cards and practice arm tapping for the following words: *and* and *the*.

Name: _____  Date: _____

# Consonants *p* & *b*

Read each letter sound below.

| | | | | | | |
|---|---|---|---|---|---|---|
| P | b | p | B | b | P | P |
| B | p | P | b | P | P | b |
| P | P | B | b | P | B | b |

Draw a circle around the pictures that begin with the letter *p*. Draw a square around the pictures that begin with the letter *b*.

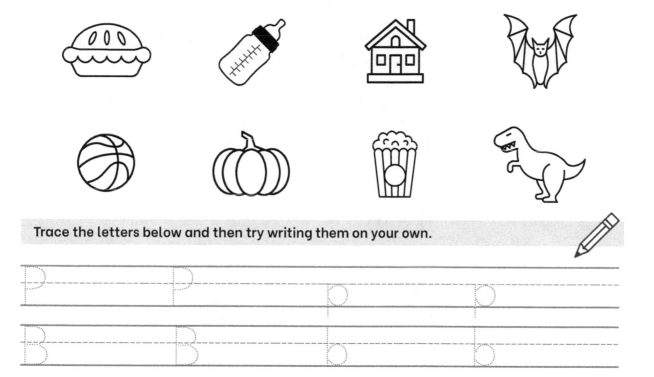

Trace the letters below and then try writing them on your own.

# Lesson 2 | Consonants *t* & *d*

## *Review*

Review letters and sounds from Lesson 1. See Ideas for Review on page 9 for suggestions.

## Introduce the New Concept

Today, students will learn two consonant sounds. Encourage them to listen to the initial sounds in the following words:

| *t* | *d* |
|-----|-----|
| tree | dinosaur |
| turtle | doll |
| tiny | dig |

To make these letter sounds, instruct students to release a puff of air while also touching their tongue to the backs of their teeth. To make a /d/ sound, tell them to make the same mouth movement, but this time, instead of just releasing air, they should release the sound from their throats. Encourage students to put their hands on their throats so they can feel the movement when they make the /t/ sound. Then have them switch between making the unvoiced /t/ and the voiced /d/ sound while still keeping a hand on their throat to feel the difference.

## Letter Sound Connections

Ask students to listen to the following list of words. After each one, encourage them to give you a thumbs up or a thumbs down if they hear the sound of the letter you are practicing.

| *t* | *d* |
|-----|-----|
| bus | dog |
| toss | dollar |
| tunnel | fan |
| cat | dill |
| trip | wash |

## Concept-Picture Connection

Guide Word(s): tree, dinosaur

## Multisensory Connections

Ask students to listen to the following sounds or initial letter sounds in the words. Instruct them to write the letter in their tactile material. This section includes sounds from previous lessons in addition to the new concept.

| | |
|---|---|
| *T* | trick |
| *b* | tip |
| *p* | pony |
| *D* | drop |
| *d* | butter |
| *t* | dinosaur |

## Sight Words

Create index cards and practice arm tapping for the following words: *be* and *look.*

# Consonants *t* & *d*

**Read each letter sound below.**

| T | d | D | B | P | d | T | D |
| B | b | p | t | T | d | D | b |
| B | t | P | b | P | P | b | D |

**What is the initial sound you hear for each picture? Write the letter *t* or *d* above it.**

_____          _____          _____          _____

**Trace the letters below and then try writing them on your own.**

# Lesson 3 | Consonants *k* & *g*

*Review*

## Introduce the New Concept

Today, students will learn two consonant sounds. Encourage them to listen to the initial sounds in the following words:

| *k* | *g* |
|---|---|
| kangaroo | gum |
| kiss | gorilla |
| kite | girl |

To make these letter sounds, instruct students to release a puff of air while touching their tongue to the roof of their mouth. To demonstrate, have students put their fingers on their tongue. Tell them to try making the /k/ or /g/ sound. They will not be able to without the movement of their tongue! Have students practice alternating between the unvoiced /k/ and voiced /g/ sound.

Be aware that students may come up with words that start with the /k/ sound but are spelled with *c*. Let them know that they are hearing the correct sound, but the word is spelled with a *c* because *c* can also make that sound. They will learn more about this later in this unit.

## Letter Sound Connections

Ask students to listen to the following words. After each one, encourage them to give you a thumbs up or a thumbs down if they hear the sound of the letter you are practicing.

| *k* | *g* |
|---|---|
| kit | gust |
| nut | mall |
| pop | zip |
| kid | gills |

## Concept-Picture Connection

Guide Word(s): kit, grapes

## Multisensory Connections

Tell students to listen to the following sounds or initial letter sounds in the words. Instruct them to write the letter in their tactile material. This section includes sounds from previous lessons in addition to the new concept.

| | | |
|---|---|---|
| K | gust | dig |
| g | kettle | pink |
| p | tree | bud |
| d | grapes | gorilla |
| t | kite | kid |

## Sight Words

Create index cards and practice arm tapping for the following words: *said* and *you*.

# Consonants *k & g*

**Read each letter sound below.**

| | | | | | | | |
|---|---|---|---|---|---|---|---|
| T | d | K | B | g | G | t | D |
| G | b | p | g | T | K | D | k |
| K | t | g | G | P | k | G | B |

**What is the initial sound you hear for each picture? Write the letter *k* or *g* above it.**

_____    _____    _____    _____

**Trace the letters below and then try writing them on your own.**

K    K    K    K

G    G    g    g

# Lesson 4 | Short *i*

*Review*

## Introduce the New Concept

During this lesson, students will learn their first vowel sound. Encourage them to listen to the initial sounds and medial sounds in the following words:

| initial short *i* | medial short *i* |
|:---:|:---:|
| igloo | pit |
| image | dip |
| introduce | big |

To make this vowel sound, ask students to keep their lips relaxed and make a tiny smile. Instruct them to watch your mouth and nose as you make this sound. Then teach them to make an exaggerated /i/ sound by putting their index finger on their nose. They can crunch their nose (like a rabbit) while making the sound. In the future, if students are struggling to remember this vowel sound, model the rabbit nose crunching as a reminder.

## Letter Sound Connections

Instruct students to listen to the following list of words. After each one, encourage them to give you a thumbs up or a thumbs down if they hear the sound of the letter you are practicing.

| initial short *i* | medial short *i* |
|:---:|:---:|
| igloo | pig |
| happy | pod |
| inner | hip |
| ill | rim |
| apple | duck |

## Finger Tapping

As a reminder, tap once for each sound.

| big | 3 taps | b-i-g |
|:---:|:---:|:---:|
| kit | 3 taps | k-i-t |
| tip | 3 taps | t-i-p |

## Elkonin Boxes

Model how to write the following words in Elkonin boxes. As a reminder, only one sound goes in each box.

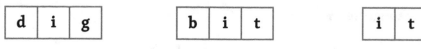

| d | i | g |
|---|---|---|

| b | i | t |
|---|---|---|

| i | t |
|---|---|

Next, instruct your students to use blank Elkonin boxes to write the following words:

kit                          big                          dip

## Concept-Picture Connection

Guide Word(s): igloo

## Multisensory Connections

Have your students listen to the following sounds or initial letter sounds in the words. Ask them to write the letter using their tactile material. This section includes sounds from previous lessons in addition to the new concept.

| *i* | big | kite |
|-----|-----|------|
| *k* | igloo | gut |
| *p* | top | iguana |
| *g* | inch | ill |
| *t* | image | dinosaur |

## Sight Words

Create index cards and practice arm tapping for the following words: *can, go,* and *I.*

## Mini Assessment

Ask your students to spell the following words: *tip* and *it.*

# Short *i*

**Read each letter sound below.**

| | | | | | |
|---|---|---|---|---|---|
| i | d | K | l | g | G |
| i | k | K | T | D | t |

**Read each real and nonsense word below.**

| | | |
|---|---|---|
| kip | big | kit |
| dig | bit | bib |
| dip | kig | tip |
| bid | kid | tib |

**Circle the pictures below that have an initial short *i* sound.**

**Circle the pictures below that have a medial short *i* sound.**

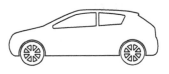

**Trace the letters below and then try writing them on your own.**

Name: _____  Date: _____

# Mini Assessment #1

**Read the following letter sounds:**

| k | g | i | t | d | b | p |
|---|---|---|---|---|---|---|

kip                dig                tid                bit

**Spelling: Try your best to spell each word you hear.**

_____

_____

## Lesson 5 | Consonants *f* & *v*

*Review*

### Introduce the New Concept

This lesson introduces students to the consonant sounds for *f* and *v*. Encourage your class to listen to the initial sounds in the following words:

| *f* | *v* |
|---|---|
| fun | van |
| fig | video |
| fly | valley |

These sounds are called "lip coolers." To make the *f* sound, which is considered an unvoiced "lip cooler," put your teeth a tiny bit over the bottom lip, stick out your lips, and then release the air. It should feel like a burst of air passing through your narrowed lips. To make the voiced *v*, make the same mouth movement, but release the sound from your throat. Model these mouth movements for your students to mimic.

### Letter Sound Connections

Students should listen to the following list of words. After each one, encourage them to give you a thumbs up or a thumbs down if they hear the sound of the letter you are practicing.

| initial *f* | initial *v* |
|---|---|
| fast | vast |
| fill | cob |
| vital | vermin |
| family | vendor |
| flamingo | fad |

### Finger Tapping

| fin | 3 taps | f-i-n |
|---|---|---|
| fit | 3 taps | f-i-t |
| fig | 3 taps | f-i-g |

## Elkonin Boxes

Model how to write the following words in Elkonin boxes.

  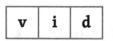

Next, instruct your students to use blank Elkonin boxes to write the following words:

fin                fig                vid

## Concept-Picture Connection

Guide Word(s): flower, van

## Multisensory Connections

Tell students to listen to the following sounds or initial letter sounds in the words. Instruct them to write the letter using their tactile material. This section includes sounds from previous lessons in addition to the new concept.

| | | |
|---|---|---|
| *i* | vacuum | bit |
| *f* | far | dog |
| *p* | kid | dill |
| *v* | gust | furniture |
| *t* | video | fuss |

## Sight Words

Create index cards and practice arm tapping for the following words: *so*, *do*, and *we*.

# Consonants *f* & *v*

**Read each letter sound and word below.**

| | | | | | |
|---|---|---|---|---|---|
| f | d | V | v | F | G |
| i | V | k | f | T | p |

**Read each real and nonsense word below.**

| | | |
|---|---|---|
| fit | fig | kid |
| vid | bit | dig |
| vit | big | kit |

**Trace the letters below and then try writing them on your own.**

**Cut out and then glue the pictures under their initial sound.**

| *f* | *v* |
|---|---|

# Lesson 6 | Short *e*

*Review*

## Introduce the New Concept

Students learn a new vowel sound in this lesson. Encourage your class to listen to the initial sounds and medial sounds in the following words:

| initial short *e* | medial short *e* |
|---|---|
| elephant | pet |
| egg | leg |
| education | men |

To make this vowel sound, tell students to drop their chins slightly and make an open-mouthed smile. To emphasize this movement, have them take their dominant hand and put their thumb and pointer finger on each corner of their mouth. Then ask them to make the short /e/ sound. Model this several times to show how the corners of your mouth spread out while making the /e/ sound. Later on, if students are struggling to remember the vowel sound, you can model this "e smile by putting your thumb and index finger on each corner of your mouth.

## Letter Sound Connections

Instruct students to listen to the following list of words. After each one, encourage them to give you a thumbs up or a thumbs down if they hear the sound of the letter you are practicing.

| initial short *e* | medial short *e* |
|---|---|
| ember | bed |
| Ed | vet |
| rip | tick |
| iguana | let |
| egg | dip |

## Finger Tapping

| | | |
|---|---|---|
| egg | 2 taps | e-gg |
| fed | 3 taps | f-e-d |
| bed | 3 taps | b-e-d |

## Elkonin Boxes

Model how to write the following words in Elkonin boxes.

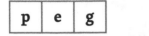  

Next, instruct your students to use blank Elkonin boxes to write the following words:

pet          bet          dip

## Concept-Picture Connection

Guide Word(s): elephant

## Multisensory Connections

Tell students to listen to the following sounds or initial letter sounds in the words. Then ask them to write the letter using their tactile material. This section includes sounds from previous lessons in addition to the new concept.

| | | |
|---|---|---|
| *e* | end | tap |
| *f* | Ellie | dill |
| *i* | kangaroo | bug |
| *v* | vet | egg |
| *k* | feed | injure |

## Sight Words

Create index cards and practice arm tapping for the following words: *by*, *a*, and *no*.

## Mini Assessment

Ask your students to spell the following words: *beg* and *dip*.

# Short *e*

**Read each letter sound below.**

| t | i | V | b | E | e | i |
|---|---|---|---|---|---|---|
| k | f | e | i | V | d | G |

**Read each word below.**

| fed | big | bid |
|-----|-----|-----|
| pet | dig | fig |
| kid | bet | vet |

**Read each sentence. Circle the short *e* words.**

1. Look at the big bed.
2. Ted fed the pig.
3. The kid did fib.

**Trace the letters below and then try writing them on your own.**

**Draw a circle around the short *e* pictures. Draw a triangle around the short *i* pictures.**

# Mini Assessment #2

**Read the following letter sounds and words:**

| k | g | e | i | t | d | b | p |
|---|---|---|---|---|---|---|---|

| vet | big | bed | kit | fig |
|---|---|---|---|---|

**Spelling: Try your best to spell each word you hear.**

1. _____

2. _____

## Lesson 7 | Consonants *s* & *z*

*Review*

### Introduce the New Concept

During this lesson, students will learn two consonant sounds. Encourage them to listen to the initial sounds in the following words:

| *s* | *z* |
|-----|-----|
| sun | zipper |
| sash | zebra |
| silly | zany |

These letters are called "skinny air letters." This is because the teeth are closed tightly and the lips part just a bit to release the sound. Students will feel their tongue touch against the back of their teeth while they make the letter sounds. /S/ is the unvoiced sound and /z/ is voiced.

Note: Some students may notice that *s* can make a /z/ sound, usually when it is positioned at the end of a word such as in *is* or *crabs*. This is covered in a later lesson.

### Letter Sound Connections

Have students listen to the following list of words. After each one, encourage them to give you a thumbs up or a thumbs down if they hear the sound of the letter you are practicing.

| initial *s* | initial *z* |
|-------------|-------------|
| sip | zest |
| cup | zigzag |
| sell | rabbit |
| sunshine | zebra |
| snake | slush |

### Finger Tapping

| | | |
|------|--------|-------|
| sit | 3 taps | s-i-t |
| zip | 3 taps | z-i-p |
| set | 3 taps | s-e-t |

## Elkonin Boxes

Model how to write the following words in Elkonin boxes.

| s | i | p |
|---|---|---|

| z | e | d |
|---|---|---|

Next, instruct your students to use blank Elkonin boxes to write the following words:

set                          zit                          sit

## Concept-Picture Connection

Guide Word(s): sun, zipper

## Multisensory Connections

Tell students to listen to the following sounds or initial letter sounds in the words. This list includes both real and nonsense words. Ask them to write the letter in their tactile material. This section includes sounds from previous lessons in addition to the new concept.

| *e* | fed | sit |
|-----|-----|-----|
| *z* | vet | zep |
| *i* | set | zid |
| *v* | zip | sib |
| *s* | pig | dip |

## Sight Words

Create index cards and practice arm tapping for the following words: *at*, *but*, and *get*.

# Consonants *s* & *z*

**Read each letter sound below.**

| f | i | Z | v | s | e |
|---|---|---|---|---|---|
| S | z | k | f | e | k |

**Read each real and nonsense word below.**

| sit | zed | get |
|-----|-----|-----|
| pet | sig | sib |
| zip | bet | vet |

**Read each sentence below.**

1. The pig did sit.
2. Zib fed the big pig.

**Trace the letters below and then try writing them on your own.**

S    S    S    S

Z    Z    Z

**In the space below, draw a picture of something that begins with the letter *s* and something that begins with the letter *z*. Label them with the letters.**

# Lesson 8 | Short a

*Review*

## Introduce the New Concept

This lesson introduces students to a new vowel sound. Encourage them to listen to the initial sounds and medial sounds in the following words:

| initial short *a* | medial short *a* |
|---|---|
| apple | mad |
| attitude | sat |
| aloe | cap |

To make this vowel sound, ask students to open their mouths and drop their chins. To emphasize this movement, put your hand flat under your chin. Then drop your chin to make the short /a/ sound. Have students try this movement. Later on, if students are struggling to remember the vowel sound, you can model the short /a/ sound by dropping your chin.

## Letter Sound Connections

Have students listen to the following list of words. After each one, encourage them to give you a thumbs up or a thumbs down if they hear the sound of the letter you are practicing.

| initial short *a* | medial short *a* |
|---|---|
| agriculture | hat |
| elephant | cat |
| adding | bed |
| inchworm | fit |
| avenue | fad |

## Finger Tapping

| | | |
|---|---|---|
| ab | 2 taps | a-b |
| bat | 3 taps | b-a-t |
| sad | 3 taps | s-a-d |

## Elkonin Boxes

Model how to write the following words in Elkonin boxes.

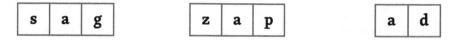

| s | a | g |
|---|---|---|

| z | a | p |
|---|---|---|

| a | d |
|---|---|

Next, instruct your students to use blank Elkonin boxes to write the following words:

pat          sat          tad

## Concept-Picture Connection

Guide Word(s): alligator

## Multisensory Connections

Tell students to listen to the following sounds or initial letter sounds in the words. Instruct them to write the letter using their tactile material.

| *e* | act | bat |
|---|---|---|
| *a* | egg | van |
| *i* | iguana | zip |
| *v* | sap | alley |
| *z* | add | fan |

## Sight Words

Create index cards and practice arm tapping for the following words: *all*, *of*, and *is*.

## Mini Assessment

Ask students to spell the following words: *sip* and *fad*.

# Short *a*

**Read each letter sound below.**

| | | | | | |
|---|---|---|---|---|---|
| A | z | D | v | E | a | i |
| S | A | f | e | a | V | l |

**Read each real and nonsense word below.**

| | | |
|---|---|---|
| fad | sat | bat |
| pig | zep | fap |
| zap | zad | bep |
| set | gab | pag |

**Read each sentence below.**

1. All of you can sit.
2. Look at the bad fad.

3. Zip the big bag.
4. "Get the fig!" said Ted.

**Trace the letters below and then try writing them on your own.**

A    A         a         a

**Circle all of the pictures that have a short *a* in the word.**

Name: _____ Date: _____

# Mini Assessment #3

**Read the following letter sounds and words:**

| k | g | e | i | t | d | b | p |
|---|---|---|---|---|---|---|---|
| | f | | v | | s | | z |

zap     fed     kit     bat

**Spelling: Try your best to spell each word you hear.**

1.

2.

# Lesson 9 | Consonants and Digraphs *ch & j*

*Review*

## Introduce the New Concept

Today's lesson teaches students about a consonant digraph and a consonant. Encourage them to listen to the initial sounds in the following words:

| *ch* | *j* |
|------|-----|
| chip | juggle |
| chunk | jump |
| child | June |

These letters are called "fat air" letters. To make the /ch/ sound, ask students to flatten their tongues and release a big burst of air across their teeth. To make the /j/ sound, instruct them to make the same mouth movement but release the sound from the throat. *Ch* is the unvoiced sound and *j* is voiced.

## Letter Sound Connections

Have students listen to the following list of words. After each one, encourage them to give you a thumbs up or a thumbs down if they hear the sound of the letter you are practicing.

| **initial** *ch* | **initial** *j* |
|------------------|-----------------|
| chocolate | chin |
| fuzz | jam |
| chimpanzee | jig |
| chill | bus |
| suds | jiggle |

## Finger Tapping

| chat | 3 taps | ch-a-t |
|------|--------|--------|
| jet | 3 taps | j-e-t |
| chip | 3 taps | ch-i-p |

## Elkonin Boxes

Model how to write the following words in Elkonin boxes.

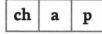

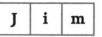

Next, instruct your students to use blank Elkonin boxes to write the following words:

chit                jab                Chad

## Concept-Picture Connection

Guide Word(s): cheese, jam

## Multisensory Connections

Tell students to listen to the following sounds or words. This list includes both real and nonsense words. Instruct them to write the letter or word in their tactile material. This section includes sounds from previous lessons in addition to the new concept.

| | | |
|---|---|---|
| *j* | Jed | sit |
| *ch* | chat | zep |
| *i* | jet | chid |
| *v* | zip | jab |
| *s* | pig | dip |

## Sight Words

Create index cards and practice arm tapping for the following words: *day*, *my*, and *to*.

# Consonants and Digraphs *ch* & *j*

**Read each letter sound below.**

| | | | | | | |
|---|---|---|---|---|---|---|
| A | z | Ch | v | i | ch | i |
| S | E | ch | e | J | V | b |

**Read each real and nonsense word below.**

| | | |
|---|---|---|
| fad | jet | zad |
| jig | sat | jab |
| chap | zep | fap |

**Read each sentence below.**

1. I chat all day.
2. Look by the jet.

3. Do you chat?
4. Chip and Chad said no.

**Trace the letters below and then try writing them on your own.**

Ch        Ch        ch        ch

J        J        j        j

**What is the initial sound you hear for each picture? Write the letters *ch* or *j* above it.**

_____   _____   _____   _____

# Lesson 10 | Consonants *m* & *n*

*Review*

## Introduce the New Concept

During this lesson, students will learn two consonants. Encourage them to listen to the initial sounds in the following words:

| *m* | *n* |
|---|---|
| monkey | neighbor |
| mild | newt |
| mother | nugget |

These letters are called "nosey" letters. This is because the sound actually comes out of your nose, not your mouth! To form the /m/ sound, ask students to close their lips tightly and then hum. To model how it comes out of your nose, have students plug their noses while they make the sound. When they plug their noses, they will no longer hear the sound clearly. To make the /n/ sound, the mouth should be slightly open while the tongue presses against the inside gums of the top teeth. Have students alternate making these sounds and plugging their noses.

## Letter Sound Connections

Ask students to listen to the following list of words. After each one, encourage them to give you a thumbs up or a thumbs down if they hear the sound of the letter you are practicing.

| initial *m* | initial *n* |
|---|---|
| map | nap |
| mom | nugget |
| kite | dress |
| mist | necklace |
| mystery | narwhal |

## Finger Tapping

| men | 3 taps | m-e-n |
|---|---|---|
| pen | 3 taps | p-e-n |
| nip | 3 taps | n-i-p |

## Elkonin Boxes

Model how to write the following words in Elkonin boxes.

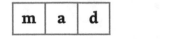    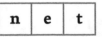

Next, instruct your students to use blank Elkonin boxes to write the following words:

Meg                              nip                              zen

## Concept-Picture Connection

Guide Word(s): monster, nest

## Multisensory Connections

Have students listen to the following sounds or words. This list includes both real and nonsense words. Ask them to write the letter or word using their tactile material. This section includes sounds from previous lessons in addition to the new concept.

| | | |
|---|---|---|
| *m* | Jim | nag |
| *ch* | pig | ned |
| *n* | zip | mad |
| *v* | bat | ven |
| *s* | chat | min |

## Sight Words

Create index cards and practice arm tapping for the following words: *she*, *he*, and *was*.

# Consonants *m* & *n*

**Read each letter sound below.**

| | | | | | | |
|---|---|---|---|---|---|---|
| A | z | M | v | m | N | i |
| S | E | ch | e | j | V | m |

**Read each real and nonsense word below.**

| | | |
|---|---|---|
| mad | zim | ten |
| in | zab | nep |
| nim | tin | nap |

**Read each sentence below.**

1. He is mad at the bad pig.
2. Ned and Tad said no.
3. "Look at the bat, Meg!"
4. She was mad at Nat.

**Trace the letters below and then try writing them on your own.**

M  M  m  m

N  N  n  n

**Circle the letter that represents the beginning sound of each picture.**

m  n        m  n        m  n

# Lesson 11 | Short o

*Review*

## Introduce the New Concept

Today, students will learn a new vowel sound. Encourage your class to listen to the initial sounds and medial sounds in the following words:

| initial short o | medial short o |
|---|---|
| olive | pot |
| operation | clock |
| octopus | fox |

To make this vowel sound, ask students to open their mouths into what looks like an *o* shape. To emphasize the movement, make a circular movement around your *o*-shaped mouth while making the sound.

## Letter Sound Connections

Instruct students to listen to the following list of words. After each one, encourage them to give you a thumbs up or a thumbs down if they hear the sound of the letter you are practicing.

| initial short o | medial short o |
|---|---|
| ostrich | cob |
| Oliver | hat |
| apple | fix |
| on | bob |
| ox | tot |

## Finger Tapping

| | | |
|---|---|---|
| bog | 3 taps | b-o-g |
| not | 3 taps | n-o-t |
| mop | 3 taps | m-o-p |

## Elkonin Boxes

Model how to write the following words in Elkonin boxes.

| j | o | t |
|---|---|---|

| p | o | p |
|---|---|---|

Next, instruct your students to use blank Elkonin boxes to write the following words:

pot                    sop                    Tom

## Concept-Picture Connection

Guide Word(s): olive

## Multisensory Connections

Tell students to listen to the following sounds or initial letter sounds. Ask them to write the letter in their tactile material.

| *m* | zom | map |
| *a* | zen | mat |
| *e* | mop | jet |
| *i* | not | set |
| *o* | bog | Meg |

## Sight Words

Create index cards and practice arm tapping for the following words: *one, two,* and *did*.

## Mini Assessment

Students should spell the following words: *fog* and *chop*.

# Short *o*

**Read each letter sound below.**

| | | | | | | |
|---|---|---|---|---|---|---|
| O | z | o | v | m | N | i |
| o | E | ch | e | j | V | m |

**Read each real and nonsense word below.**

| | | |
|---|---|---|
| not | mig | nom |
| nap | fig | dip |
| bod | fog | chap |
| chog | zop | chin |

**Read each sentence below. Circle the short *o* words.**

1. One bog is big.
2. Two pigs did jig.
3. Todd and Bob said no.
4. Chop the chip for Jen.

**Trace the letters below and then try writing them on your own.**

**Spell the word illustrated in each picture below.**

# Mini Assessment #4

**Read the following letter sounds and words:**

| k | g | m | i | t | d | a | p |
|---|---|---|---|---|---|---|---|
| ch | | v | | n | | z | e | | o |

top          Chad          job          nip

**Spelling: Try your best to spell each word you hear.**

1. _____

2. _____

# Lesson 12 | Consonants and Digraphs *w, h,* & *wh*

*Review*

## Introduce the New Concept

This lesson teaches students about two consonants and one consonant digraph. Encourage your class to listen to the initial sounds in the following words:

| *w* | *h* | *wh* |
|---|---|---|
| walrus | hug | whistle |
| waste | happy | when |
| wall | hatch | whip |

These letters are called "windy" sounds. We make each of these sounds by forcefully releasing air from the mouth when it is positioned in a specific way.

To make a /w/ sound and a /wh/ sound, start with your mouth in an *o* shape. Then release the *o* while releasing air. For spelling purposes, teach students that the *w* spelling is far more common than the *wh*. Students will learn many words with the *wh* spelling as sight words.

To form an /h/ sound, open your mouth and release a breathy stream of air. This is an unvoiced sound.

It is interesting to note that in some dialects, particularly those with Scottish, Irish, or southern US influences, the *wh* includes a breathy /h/ prior to the /w/ sound in the *wh* digraph. This is not common across the US, but you may consider changing your teaching if this pronunciation is common in your area.

## Letter Sound Connections

Have students listen to the following list of words. After each one, encourage them to give you a thumbs up or a thumbs down if they hear the sound of the letter you are practicing.

| initial *w/wh* | initial *h* |
|---|---|
| wig | host |
| whisk | huge |
| where | chip |
| goat | wax |
| wish | holly |

## Finger Tapping

| | | |
|---|---|---|
| win | 3 taps | w-i-n |
| whip | 3 taps | wh-i-p |
| hot | 3 taps | h-o-t |

## Elkonin Boxes

Model how to write the following words in Elkonin boxes.

| w | a | g |
|---|---|---|

| h | i | t |
|---|---|---|

Next, instruct your students to use blank Elkonin boxes to write the following words:

wed                    hid                    when

## Concept-Picture Connection

Guide Word(s): wing, hive, whisper

## Multisensory Connections

Tell students to listen to the following sounds or words. Encourage them to write the letter(s) or word in their tactile material. This section includes sounds from previous lessons in addition to the new concept.

| | | |
|---|---|---|
| *w/wh* | wit | him |
| *ch* | had | hop |
| *e* | whim | hen |
| *h* | win | chap |
| *o* | whip | dip |

## Sight Words

Create index cards and practice arm tapping for the following words: *when*, *which*, and *had*.

# Consonants and Digraph *w*, *h*, & *wh*

**Read each letter sound below.**

| wh | z | o | w | m | N | h |
|----|---|---|---|---|---|---|
| O | E | ch | e | j | h | wh |

**Read each real and nonsense word below.**

| whip | dip | set |
|------|-----|-----|
| hid | wag | jet |
| had | Jon | hod |
| wet | hot | whog |

**Read each sentence below.**

1. The pigs had wigs.

2. When do the dogs hop?

3. Which bat did hit?

**Trace the letters below and then try writing them on your own.**

W        W        W        W

H        H        h        h        wh

**What is the initial sound you hear for each picture? Write the letter *h* or *w* above it.**

# Lesson 13 | Consonants *l* & *r*

*Review*

## Introduce the New Concept

During this lesson, students will learn two consonants. Encourage them to listen to the initial sounds in the following words:

| *l* | *r* |
|---|---|
| lightning | roast |
| lose | runt |
| lemur | reef |

These letters are called "tongue lifter" sounds. We make each of these sounds by lifting the tongue in a specific area of the mouth. To make an /l/ sound, lift the tip of the tongue behind the back teeth. Then release the sound.

To make an /r/ sound, lift the back of the tongue toward the soft palate. Then release the sound. Model these sounds for students to mimic.

## Letter Sound Connections

Invite students to listen to the following list of words. After each one, encourage them to give you a thumbs up or a thumbs down if they hear the sound of the letter you are practicing.

| **initial *l*** | **initial *r*** |
|---|---|
| limp | right |
| stall | rabbit |
| loft | list |
| light | read |

## Finger Tapping

| rap | 3 taps | r-a-p |
|---|---|---|
| lid | 3 taps | l-i-d |
| red | 3 taps | r-e-d |

## Elkonin Boxes

Model how to write the following words in Elkonin boxes.

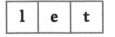
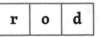

Next, instruct your students to use blank Elkonin boxes to write the following words:

rim                    log                    rat

## Concept-Picture Connection

Guide Word(s): list, railroad

## Multisensory Connections

Tell students to listen to the following sounds or words. This list includes both real and nonsense words. Instruct them to write the letter(s) or word using their tactile material. This section includes sounds from previous lessons in addition to the new concept.

| | | |
|---|---|---|
| *l* | lit | him |
| *r* | rad | lop |
| *w/wh* | rim | len |
| *h* | win | hen |
| *o* | rip | lag |

## Sight Words

Create index cards and practice arm tapping for the following words: *like*, *will*, and *see*.

# Consonants *l* & *r*

Read each letter sound and word below.

| wh | z | L | r | m | N | l |
|----|----|----|----|----|----|----|
| O | R | ch | e | i | L | m |
| lip | rid | rig | lib | rom | | rob |
| lit | rad | Jen | rag | lad | | rich |

Read each sentence below.

1. Do you see the rat in the log?
2. Will she see the pig?

3. The rig is rad.
4. Look at Rod rap.

Trace the letters below and then try writing them on your own.

Cut out and then glue the pictures below under their initial sound.

| *l* | *r* |
|-----|-----|

# Lesson 14 | Short *u*

*Review*

## Introduce the New Concept

During this lesson, students will learn a new vowel sound. Encourage your class to listen to the initial sounds and medial sounds in the following words:

| initial short *u* | medial short *u* |
|---|---|
| umbrella | pup |
| under | buck |
| ultimate | mutt |

To make this vowel sound, have students put a hand on their belly and push in slightly while releasing the sound from the mouth. The short /u/ sounds a lot like being pushed in the stomach. Model this gesture for students and use this movement to serve as a reminder for the sound.

## Letter Sound Connections

Have your students listen to the following list of words. After each one, encourage them to give you a thumbs up or a thumbs down if they hear the sound of the letter you are practicing.

| initial short *u* | medial short *u* |
|---|---|
| up | bug |
| itch | lap |
| underwear | sick |
| ash | mug |
| upper | much |

## Finger Tapping

| nut | 3 taps | n-u-t |
|---|---|---|
| hum | 3 taps | h-u-m |
| rug | 3 taps | r-u-g |

## Elkonin Boxes

Model how to write the following words in Elkonin boxes.

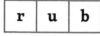          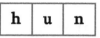

Next, instruct your students to use blank Elkonin boxes to write the following words:

|           |           |           |
|-----------|-----------|-----------|
| lug       | rug       | rub       |

## Concept-Picture Connection

Guide Word(s): umbrella

## Multisensory Connections

Tell students to listen to the following sounds or initial letter sounds. Ask them to write the letter in their tactile material.

| *u* | mug | rat  |
|-----|-----|------|
| *a* | sun | whip |
| *e* | lug | chum |
| *i* | dud | rod  |
| *o* | sud | jet  |

## Sight Words

Create index cards and practice arm tapping for the following words: *them*, *in*, *first*, and *come*.

## Mini Assessment

Instruct students to spell the following words: *chug* and *hut*.

# Short *u*

📖

**Read each letter sound below.**

| | | | | | | |
|---|---|---|---|---|---|---|
| wh | u | L | r | U | N | l |
| O | r | u | e | j | L | m |

**Read each word below.**

| | | |
|---|---|---|
| mug | but | bit |
| rut | bun | chug |
| rim | sum | him |
| set | run | dab |
| hut | hot | pun |

**Read each sentence below.**

1. Look at them run.
2. The sun is hot in the hut.

3. The rat is on the rug.
4. Look at Rod run the rig.

**Trace the letters below and then try writing them on your own.**

**Spell each word illustrated in the pictures below.**

# Mini Assessment #5

**Read the following letter sounds and words:**

| k | d | s | m | h |
|---|---|---|---|---|
| g | b | z | n | l |
| e | p | a | o | r |
| i | f | ch | w | u |
| t | v | j | wh | |

kit            fed            vet            pun

wag                rub                chop

**Spelling: Try your best to spell each word you hear.**

1. _____

2. _____

# Spelling Rule | *c, k, & -ck*

*Review*

## Introduce the New Concept

Today we will cover a spelling rule. Spelling rules are short lessons that are typically covered in one or two days. Your students have already learned the /k/ sound, so this lesson focuses strictly on the spelling patterns. Instruct your class to copy down the following spelling rules in their Orton-Gillingham notebooks.

**Hard *c* & *k*:** Hard *c* is used before consonants and the vowels *a*, *o*, and *u*. *K* is used before *e* and *i*.

**-*ck*:** -*ck* is used at the end of a one-syllable word right after a short vowel. Use *k* in all other instances.

For Advanced Students: Students have not learned syllabication concepts. However, advanced students may notice that -*c* can go at the end of two-syllable words ending in the /k/ sound. Examples of this include words such as mimic and panic.

## Elkonin Boxes

Model how to write the following words in Elkonin boxes.

Next, instruct your students to use blank Elkonin boxes to write the following words:

       cap             Kim             rock

## Concept-Picture Connection

Guide Word(s): cat, kit, duck

## Multisensory Connections

Tell students to listen to the following words and then write them using their tactile material.

       cog             sock             mock
       sick             cat             kid

# Spelling Rule *c*, *k*, & *-ck*

**Read each letter sound below.**

| c | u | L | r | -ck | N | l |
|---|---|---|---|-----|---|---|
| c | R | u | e | C | L | -ck |

**Read each word below.**

| cud | kid | sick |
|-----|-----|------|
| rock | tuck | cat |
| cot | Rick | Kim |
| kit | luck | cup |

**Trace and write the letters below.**

c          k          c     k          k

**Spell the word illustrated in each picture below.**

lo_____     _____ap     _____ick

# Lesson 15 | Consonant *x*

*Review*

## Introduce the New Concept

Today students will learn about a consonant that makes several sounds. Encourage your class to listen to the final sounds in the following words:

*x*

fox

six

box

mix

The letter *x* is known as a "borrower" because it can make multiple sounds. Its most common sound by far, and the sound covered in this lesson, sounds like a blend of /k/ and /s/ as in the word fox. X can also sound like a /z/ as in xylophone and /gz/ as in exist. The last two patterns are not explicitly taught in this text since they are relatively rare, but it is helpful to teach students that *x* can have multiple sounds. Model the sounds above for students to mimic.

## Letter Sound Connections

Invite students to listen to the following list of words. After each one, encourage them to give you a thumbs up or a thumbs down if they hear the sound of the letter you are practicing.

*x*

box

six

mix

lox

Challenge: exit, exercise

## Finger Tapping

| | | |
|---|---|---|
| pox | 3 taps | p-o-x |
| lox | 3 taps | l-o-x |
| max | 3 taps | m-a-x |

## Elkonin Boxes

Model how to write the following words in Elkonin boxes.

| s | i | x |
|---|---|---|

| b | o | x |
|---|---|---|

Next, instruct your students to use blank Elkonin boxes to write the following words:

mix                    lox                    fox

## Concept-Picture Connection

Guide Word(s): fox, xylophone*, exist*

*There is no need to make cards for *xylophone* and *exist*. These concepts are strictly to inform students that *x* can make multiple sounds.

## Multisensory Connections

Tell students to listen to the following sounds or words and then write the letter or word in their tactile material. This section includes sounds from previous lessons in addition to the new concept.

| | | |
|---|---|---|
| *u* | mix | box |
| *r* | lox | sick |
| *l* | six | fix |
| *h* | wax | pox |
| *e* | lock | nick |

## Sight Words

Create index cards and practice arm tapping for the following words: *not, have, this,* and *it.*

# Consonant *x*

**Read each letter sound below.**

| c | u | x | r | -ck | N | l |
|---|---|---|---|-----|---|---|
| X | R | u | e | x | L | -ck |

**Read each real and nonsense word below.**

| | | |
|---|---|---|
| mix | huck | cud |
| box | lox | luck |
| Rick | wax | fox |
| wix | Chex | rock |
| ox | nix | cub |

**Read each sentence below.**

1. I have a big box.
2. The fox did not go on the box.
3. Rick had the lox.

4. I have six socks.
5. The fox did not like the ox.

**Trace the letters below and then try writing them on your own.**

**Color the pictures that have the /x/ sound.**

# Lesson 16 | Consonant *y*

*Review*

## Introduce the New Concept

During this lesson, students will learn one consonant. Encourage them to listen to the initial sounds in the following words:

**consonant *y***

yellow

yes

young

yell

The letter *y* is an interesting letter because it can make both a consonant sound and a vowel sound. The consonant *y* is formed by starting with the mouth open with the tongue touching the roof of the mouth. Then, open the mouth wider while you release the sound. Model this sound for students to mimic.

*Y* can also make three vowel sounds of e and i as in scary, fry, and gym. These are reviewed in Unit 6 on page 197.

## Letter Sound Connections

Have students listen to the following list of words. After each one, encourage them to give you a thumbs up or a thumbs down if they hear the sound of the letter you are practicing.

**initial *y***

yuck

valley

yurt

yum

pool

## Finger Tapping

| | | |
|---|---|---|
| yap | 3 taps | y-a-p |
| yet | 3 taps | y-e-t |
| yuck | 3 taps | y-u-ck |

## Elkonin Boxes

Model how to write the following words in Elkonin boxes.

| y | u | m |
|---|---|---|

| y | e | s |
|---|---|---|

Next, instruct your students to use blank Elkonin boxes to write the following words:

yon                              yup                              yap

## Concept-Picture Connection

Guide Word(s): yak

## Multisensory Connections

Tell students to listen to the following sounds and words and then write the letter(s) or word using their tactile material. This section includes sounds from previous lessons in addition to the new concept.

| | | |
|---|---|---|
| *y* | yip | lox |
| *x* | mix | yuck |
| *r* | yap | yum |
| *u* | yet | nix |
| *-ck* | yon | yup |

## Sight Words

Create index cards and practice arm tapping for the following words: *on* and make.

# Consonant y

**Read each letter sound below.**

| c | Y | x | y | -ck | N | Y |
|---|---|---|---|-----|---|---|
| X | R | u | e | y   | L | -ck |

**Read each real and nonsense word below.**

| yet | yes | yit |
|-----|-----|-----|
| yak | fox | yix |
| yon | yum | pex |
| luck | yuck | beck |

**Read each sentence below.**

1. I like the dog, but he yaps.
2. The yak did yap.
3. Yes, she will.

4. Did you see Jon yet?
5. Do not yip at the yak.

**Trace the letters below and then try writing them on your own.**

**Circle the letter of the beginning sound for each picture.**

P
Y
K

A
R
P

Y
L
Z

# Lesson 17 | Digraph *qu*

## *Review*

## Introduce the New Concept

This lesson teaches students about another consonant. Encourage them to listen to the initial sound in the following words:

**qu**

queen

quiz

quick

quell

The letter *q* is unique because it rarely appears in an English word without *u*! This is why it is taught as a *qu* rather than just a *q*.

To emphasize this point, you may want to have a "*q* and *u* wedding" to show that the letters are always together!

*Q* can actually make two sounds. In its most common form, *q* sounds like a *k* and *w* blended together. The sound starts from the throat. Then you open your mouth into an *o* shape to let the sound out. Model this sound for students to mimic.

*Q* can also make the sound of *k* in words like unique and clique. This is covered in Unit 9.

## Letter Sound Connections

Ask students to listen to the following list of words. After each one, encourage them to give you a thumbs up or a thumbs down if they hear the sound of the letter you are practicing.

**initial qu**

quiz

quit

yellow

Quinn

waste

## Finger Tapping

| | | |
|---|---|---|
| quid | 3 taps | qu-i-d |
| quiz | 3 taps | qu-i-z |
| quick | 3 taps | qu-i-ck |

## Elkonin Boxes

Model how to write the following words in Elkonin boxes.

| qu | e | ll |
|---|---|---|

| qu | i | t |
|---|---|---|

Next, instruct your students to use blank Elkonin boxes to write the following words:

| quill | quip | quid |
|---|---|---|

## Concept-Picture Connection

Guide Word(s): question

## Multisensory Connections

Tell students to listen to the following sounds and words. This list includes both real and nonsense words. Then instruct students to write the letter(s) or word using their tactile material. This section includes sounds from previous lessons in addition to the new concept.

| | | |
|---|---|---|
| *y* | yap | rack |
| *x* | quid | cap |
| *qu* | quiz | quap |
| *k* | yes | nix |
| *l* | fox | yum |

## Sight Words

Create index cards and practice arm tapping for the following words: *down, how,* and *or.*

# Digraph *qu*

**Read each letter sound below.**

| | | | | | | |
|---|---|---|---|---|---|---|
| qu | Y | x | y | -ck | N | Qu |
| X | R | u | e | y | L | qu |

**Read each real and nonsense word below.**

| | | |
|---|---|---|
| quell | Quinn | lob |
| yip | quit | quib |
| quid | fix | zen |
| yet | luck | pack |

**Read each sentence below.**

1. Will you do the quiz?
2. Quinn had to quit.
3. Look at the quiz.
4. Quinn had the quid.

**Trace the letters below and then try writing them on your own.**

Qu          Qu

qu          qu

**Circle the pictures that begin with *qu*. Cross out the ones that don't.**

## Lesson 18 | Soft *th* & Hard *th*

*Review*

## Introduce the New Concept

Today, students are introduced to a consonant digraph that can make two sounds. Encourage your class to listen to the initial sounds in the following words:

| soft *th* | hard *th* |
|-----------|-----------|
| think | there |
| thought | them |
| throw | the |

To make each of these sounds, the tongue goes between the teeth as you expel air. The soft *th* is unvoiced and the hard *th* is voiced.

The soft *th* is the more common sound for this pattern. We typically see the hard *th* in front of words that are taught as sight words. Model each of the *th* sounds for students to mimic.

## Letter Sound Connections

Instruct students to listen to the following list of words. After each one, encourage them to give you a thumbs up or a thumbs down if they hear the sound of the letter.

| soft *th* | hard *th* |
|-----------|-----------|
| thumb | them |
| think | thin |
| top | there |
| thimble | this |
| then | toss |

## Finger Tapping

| with | 3 taps | w-i-th |
|------|--------|--------|
| then | 3 taps | th-e-n |
| thick | 3 taps | th-i-ck |

## Elkonin Boxes

Model how to write the following words in Elkonin boxes.

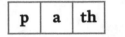

| p | a | th |
|---|---|----|

| th | e | m |
|----|---|---|

Next, instruct your students to use blank Elkonin boxes to write the following words:

bath                    math                    this

## Concept-Picture Connection

Guide Word(s): thunder, there

## Multisensory Connections

Tell students to listen to the following sounds and words and then write the letter(s) or word using their tactile material. This section includes sounds from previous lessons in addition to the new concept.

| | | |
|---|---|---|
| *qu* | quiz | quid |
| soft *th* | thin | than |
| hard *th* | thud | yet |
| *u* | this | math |
| *w* | thick | luck |

## Sight Words

Create index cards and practice arm tapping for the following words: *with*, *may*, and *then*.

# Soft *th* & Hard *th*

**Read each letter sound below.**

| qu | th | x | Th | -ck | th | Qu |
|----|----|---|----|-----|----|----|
| X | R | u | e | Th | L | y |

**Read each real and nonsense word below.**

| then | bath | them |
|------|------|------|
| this | math | thid |
| thin | Beth | yath |
| with | path | quith |

**Read each sentence below.**

1. Come with the pig, Beth.
2. The rat is in the bath.
3. Do the math, Rick.

4. Look at them go!
5. The thin cat will have a nap.

**Trace the letters below and then try writing them on your own.**

Th          Th          th          th

**Circle the pictures that have the /th/ sound.**

# Lesson 19 | Consonant Digraph *sh* & *zsh* (sound only)

*Review*

## Introduce the New Concept

Today, students will learn another consonant digraph, *sh*. They will also review the hard version of this sound, but will not be expected to read or spell words with the /zsh/ sound until later on in this text. Encourage students to listen to the sounds in the following words:

| *sh* | /zsh/ |
|------|-------|
| shop | measure |
| shrink | cashmere |
| wish | beige |

To make the sound, ask students to close their teeth and part their lips. The tongue will touch the top of the mouth while expelling air. The soft sound is unvoiced while the hard sound is voiced. Model both of these sounds for students to mimic.

## Letter Sound Connections

Have students listen to the following list of words. After each one, encourage them to give you a thumbs up or a thumbs down if they hear the sound of the letter you are practicing.

| soft *sh* | hard *sh* |
|-----------|-----------|
| shift | division |
| shrill | treasure |
| shout | television |
| fish | occasion |
| crush | leisure |

## Finger Tapping

| ship | 3 taps | sh-i-p |
|------|--------|--------|
| mesh | 3 taps | m-e-sh |
| shack | 3 taps | sh-a-ck |

## Elkonin Boxes

Model how to write the following words in Elkonin boxes.

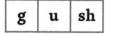   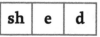

Next, instruct your students to use blank Elkonin boxes to write the following words:

mush                    fish                    shop

## Concept-Picture Connection

Guide Word(s): shell, measure

## Multisensory Connections

Tell students to listen to the following sounds and words. This list includes both real and nonsense words. Instruct your class to write the letter(s) or word using their tactile material. This section includes sounds from previous lessons in addition to the new concept.

| | | |
|---|---|---|
| soft *sh* | ship | mush |
| hard *sh* | wish | sick |
| soft *th* | shig | chip |
| hard *th* | shod | whip |
| *w* | posh | pick |

## Sight Words

Create index cards and practice arm tapping for the following words: *than*, *out*, and *more*.

Name: _____ Date: _____

# Consonant Digraph *sh* & *zsh*

**Read each letter sound below.**

| sh | th | x | Sh | -ck | th | Qu |
|----|----|---|----|-----|----|----|
| X | sh | u | e | Th | L | y |

**Read each word below.**

| shin | ship | gush |
|------|------|------|
| thin | josh | nix |
| wish | mash | bash |
| this | hush | lush |
| shack | with | gash |

**Read each sentence below.**

1. I wish for a red ship.
2. I like this ship more than that ship.
3. Can we shop for a shed?

4. Look at the fish go!
5. The mush is in the cup.

**Trace the letters below and then try writing them on your own.**

Sh      Sh      sh      sh

**Circle the pictures that have a /sh/ sound.**

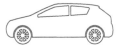 

## Spelling Rule | The Doubling Rule *ff, ss, ll, zz*

*Review*

### Introduce the New Concept

As a reminder spelling rules are short lessons that are typically covered in one to two days. Students have already learned the /s/, /l/, /f/, and /z/ sounds, so this lesson focuses on spelling with these letters at the ends of words. Instruct students to copy down the following spelling rules in their Orton-Gillingham notebooks.

**The Doubling Rule:** If a word ends with a short vowel followed by *f, l, s,* or *z,* double it!

*Exceptions*: Words such as gross, his, bus, gal, and chef.

### Elkonin Boxes

Model how to write the following words in Elkonin boxes.

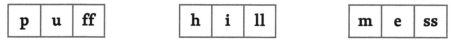

Next, instruct your students to use blank Elkonin boxes to write the following words:

| doll | buzz | miss |

### Concept-Picture Connection

Guide Word(s): kiss

### Multisensory Connections

Tell students to listen to the following words and then write them using their tactile material.

| fuzz | huff | kiss |
| will | fuzz | puff |

# The Doubling Rule *ff*, *ss*, *ll*, *zz*

**Read each letter sound below.**

| w | o | ss | sh | -ck | zz | a |
|---|---|----|----|----|----|----|
| ll | u | ff | i | e | x | ch |

**Read each word below.**

| pass | jazz | mess |
|------|------|------|
| doll | fizz | tell |
| mill | cuff | tiff |
| tell | hill | buff |
| toss | less | puff |

**Read each sentence below.**

1. Pass the doll to Bill.
2. The fizz will pop.
3. Tell me when you go to the hut.
4. The cuff on that leg is a mess.
5. Go down the hill to the mill.

**Spell the word illustrated in each picture below.**

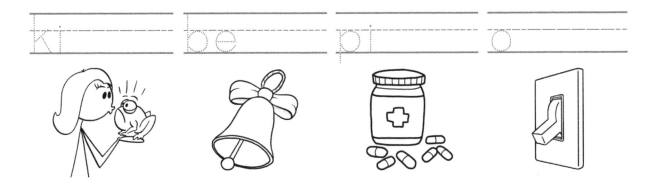

# Spelling Rule | Plural Spelling Rule -*s*, -*es*, -*lves*

*Review*

## Introduce the New Concept

Today, students will learn another spelling rule that is typically covered in one or two days.

Instruct your class to copy down the following spelling rules in their Orton-Gillingham notebooks.

**Plural Spelling Rules:**

- If a word ends with -*sh*, -*ch*, *x*, *s*, *z*, or a consonant plus *o*, add -*es*.
- If a word ends in *f*, change it to *v* and add -*es*.
- For all other words, add -*s*.
- When a word ends in *s*, the *s* may sound like /s/ or /z/.

*Exceptions*: This rule does not apply to irregular nouns such as mouse-mice, tooth-teeth, foot-feet, man-men, fish, sheep, or deer.

## Concept-Picture Connection

Guide Word(s): frogs, halves, wishes

## Multisensory Connections

Tell students to listen to the following words and then write them using their tactile material.

| | | |
|---|---|---|
| frogs | kisses | foxes |
| halves | bushes | runs |

# Plural Spelling Rule -*s*, -*es*, -*lves*

**Read each word below.**

| | | |
|---|---|---|
| cats | pods | mashes |
| taxes | tiffs | chips |
| buses | gives | kisses |
| pigs | dogs | ticks |
| calves | thins | bats |

**Read the sentences below.**

1. The cats are down by the bog.
2. The pigs and calves are buds.
3. Will the bugs nip?

4. When will you do the taxes?
5. He mashes the chips for me.

**Spell each word in its plural form.**

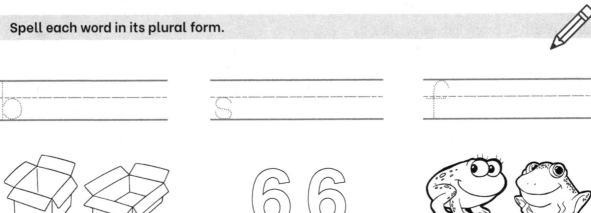

b _____    s _____    f _____

# Unit 1 Decodable Story
# The Pig's Wig

**Read the story below and then answer the questions.**

Look at the big pig. He has a red wig.

Pig likes to rock his wig. He likes to look at his big, red wig. He likes to do a jig in his wig.

Pig will go to Bug's hut with his wig. Bug will see the wig and like it. Bug said, May I have that wig?"

"No," Pig said. "This is my wig, and I like it a lot!"

Pig and Bug will go shop for a wig for Bug. The shop will have a fab wig for Bug. Pig and Bug will do jigs and hops in the wigs. That will be lots of fun!

**1.** Did Bug like Pig's wig? How can you tell?

_____

_____

_____

**2.** How did Bug get a wig?

_____

_____

_____

# Unit 1 Post-Test

**Try your best to read these words.**

| | | |
|---|---|---|
| bit | quiz | dog |
| mat | kiss | fed |
| tip | fizz | cup |
| path | lock | yes |

**Try your best to read these sentences.**

1. Did you have the fish or the duck?

2. Come get the big, red socks.

3. You can hug the pig, but do not kiss it!

4. First, we can get the rug, then we can get the bed.

**Try your best to spell the words of the picture below.**

_____     _____

_____     _____

**Circle the pictures that rhyme.**

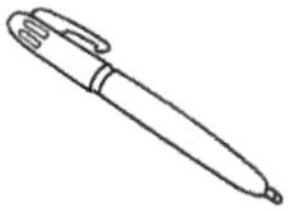

10

# Unit 2: Blends and Glued Sounds

## Tips, Tricks, and Things to Know

In this unit, students learn how to read and spell words with consonant blends and glued sounds such as *-am*, *-an*, *-all*, *-ng* and, *-nk*. This unit also covers two spelling rules, *-ct* endings and *ch/-tch*.

### Finger Tapping

When tapping a consonant blend, each letter should be tapped so long as it makes its own sound. Students may get consonant digraphs and consonant blends confused when they begin these lessons. It is important to point out that consonant digraphs such as *ch*, *sh*, *th*, and *wh* all make one sound, while consonant blends such as *bl*, *tr*, and *sk* maintain their individual letter sounds. As a reminder from Unit 1, sounds like /-ck/, /ss/, /ff/, /ll/, and /zz/ are all one tap because they make one sound.

Here are some examples:

| | | |
|---|---|---|
| grab | 4 taps | g-r-a-b |
| splash | 5 taps | s-p-l-a-sh |
| bond | 4 taps | b-o-n-d |
| grass | 4 taps | g-r-a-ss |

In the glued sounds (*-an*, *-am*, *-all*, *-ng*, and *-nk*), the sounds are kept together when tapping. This is because the vowels in words with these patterns are influenced to make a different sound. When finger tapping, students should use the number of fingers in the glued sound. For example, when tapping the word ball, right-handed students should use their pinky to tap /b/ and their ring, middle, and index fingers "glued together" to tap /all/. This is a total of two taps, but with four fingers.

Here are some examples:

| | | |
|---|---|---|
| yam | 2 taps | y-am |
| span | 3 taps | s-p-an |
| call | 2 taps | c-all |
| string | 4 taps | s-t-r-ing |
| honk | 2 taps | h-onk |

## Elkonin Boxes

The same finger-tapping rules above apply to Elkonin boxes. Here are a few examples:

| c | l | a | sh |
|---|---|---|---|
| f | o | n | d |
| p | an | | |
| s | l | am | |

| c | all | |
|---|---|---|
| s | t | ing |
| p | ink | |

## Spelling Rules

**-ct Rule:** If there is a /kt/ sound at the end of a word, it is spelled with a -ct. Words are never spelled with a -kt ending.

**-ch/-tch:** When a word ends in the /ch/ sound, use -tch if it follows a short vowel. Use -ch if it comes after a long vowel or consonant.

*Exceptions*: much, such, rich, and attach.

## Guide Words

These are the guide words used in the lessons for this unit. Guide words are a visual representation that highlight the taught skill. Use these words when referring to a specific skill. By the end of the unit, students will have a total of 19 Concept-Word Connection Cards with these guide words.

Lesson:

1. Initial 2-Letter Blends: crab
2. Initial 3-Letter Blends: splash, shrub
3. Final Blends: mask

   Spelling Rule -*ct* Ending: collect

   Spelling Rule *ch/-tch:* beach, lunch, catch
4. *am/an*: jam, pan
5. -*all*: ball
6. -*ng*: king, gong, lung, bang
7. -*nk*: rink, honk, bunk, sank

## Sight Words

Here are the sight words covered in this unit: *what, up, from, who, as, her, an, his, for, if, your, that, are, use, him, there, has, sit, been,* and *many.*

# Unit 2 Pretest

**Read the following words:**

| | | |
|---|---|---|
| snap | match | fall |
| chill | flank | clam |
| scrub | clung | pact |
| man | song | grasp |
| chalk | risk | stench |

**Read the following sentences:**

1. Use the ball to hit the spot on the dunk tank.

2. Do you have a plan for the ham?

3. I can act as strong as a ram.

4. Do not pinch the small cat.

**Try your best to spell the words of the pictures below.**

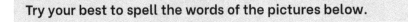

**Circle the pictures that rhyme.**

# Practice Literacy at Home

Dear Parents/Guardians,

Today, we start our journey into Unit 2: Blends and Glued Sounds. Blends are two or more letters that blend together in a word, but each letter sound can be heard. For example, in the word crab, the *cr* is a blend—you can hear both the /c/ and the /r/ sounds. Halfway

through this unit, your child will learn two spelling rules. The first is the *-ct* rule. It states that if there is a /kt/ sound at the end of a word, it is spelled with a *-ct*. The second is the *-ch* and *-tch* rule. It states that when a word ends in the /ch/ sound, use *-tch* if it follows a short vowel and use *-ch* if it comes after a long vowel or consonant. Glued sounds, also known as welded sounds, are groups of letters that are easier to learn as a chunk rather than as separate elements. For example, for the word ball, you'd pronounce the /b/ sound plus the /all/ sound instead of pronouncing each letter sound individually.

If you'd like your child to practice this unit at home, here are the dates for each lesson and some words your child can practice reading, writing, and spelling.

| Dates: | | | | | | | | |
|---|---|---|---|---|---|---|---|---|
| Skills: | Initial 2-letter blends | Initial 3-letter blends | Final blends | *-ct, -ch, & -tch* ending | Glued sounds: *-am, -an* | Glued sounds: *-al, -all* | Glued sounds: *-ng* | Glued sounds: *-nk* |
| Examples: | flat<br>spot<br>crib<br>Fred<br>slug<br>slip | splat<br>scrub<br>strut<br>stress<br>squid<br>split | test<br>silk<br>soft<br>crust<br>task<br>blend | pact<br>bench<br>glitch<br>strict<br>much<br>splotch | scam<br>ban<br>tram<br>fan<br>cram<br>plan | fall<br>chalk<br>squall<br>mall<br>ball<br>malt | strong<br>sing<br>slung<br>bang<br>bring<br>flung | bank<br>think<br>honk<br>funk<br>sink<br>rank |

To make reading and writing even more fun, have your child use Play-Doh, colored markers, or pencils to spell each word. They can even pick some of the words to draw and label!

Happy learning!

# Lesson 1 | Initial 2-Letter Blends

*Review and Pretest*

## Introduce the New Concept

Today, students will learn about consonant blends. These patterns are different from consonant digraphs like *ch*, *sh*, *wh*, and *th* because the letters in a consonant blend maintain their own sound while working together to make the sound of the blend. The letters in a digraph make a totally new sound when they are together.

Demonstrate by comparing the words below. Emphasize that the words with a consonant digraph have a sound that cannot be separated, while the ones with a consonant blend have 2 distinct (blended) letter sounds.

| consonant digraph | initial blend |
|:---:|:---:|
| ship | snap |
| chill | trick |
| thin | plug |

## Finger Tapping

Have your students practice tapping these words:

| | | |
|:---:|:---:|:---:|
| glad | 4 taps | g-l-a-d |
| thick | 3 taps | th-i-ck |
| snack | 4 taps | s-n-a-ck |

## Elkonin Boxes

Model how to write the following words in Elkonin boxes.

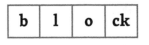

| b | l | o | ck |
|:---:|:---:|:---:|:---:|

| s | w | i | m |
|:---:|:---:|:---:|:---:|

Next, instruct your students to use blank Elkonin boxes to write the following words:

| | | |
|:---:|:---:|:---:|
| twin | shin | frill |
| scum | spot | plush |

## Concept-Picture Connection

Guide Word(s): crab

## Multisensory Connections

| slip | grip | black | snap | crop |
|------|------|-------|------|------|
| drop | flat | shin | class | grill |

## Sight Words

Create index cards and practice arm tapping for the following words: *what* and *up*.

## Mini Assessment

Ask your students to spell the following words: *trip*, *spin*, *swish*, and *pluck*.

Name: _____  Date:_____

# Initial 2-Letter Blends

**Read each word below.**

## Real Words

| | | |
|---|---|---|
| crab | dress | plus |
| crop | drop | plug |
| grass | black | scab |
| grab | click | twin |
| frog | flat | snack |

## Nonsense Words

| | | |
|---|---|---|
| plob | slib | spog |
| trid | greb | dran |

**Read each sentence below.**

1. Do you see the sled slip?
2. The frog did not see the crab in the grass.
3. The black spot was on the snack.
4. Can you spin the flag?
5. Did you see the clock in the class?

# Initial 2-Letter Blends
# Mini Assessment

**Read the following words:**

| crib | frill | clock |
|------|-------|-------|
| prim | slum | glum |
| trot | drum | flag |
| grit | block | glad |

**Spelling: Try your best to spell each word you hear.**

1. _____

2. _____

3. _____

4. _____

# Lesson 2 | Initial 3-Letter Blends

*Review*

## Introduce the New Concept

Today, students will learn to blend words that have 3-letter consonant blends. There are fewer words with this pattern than 2-letter consonant blends. In addition, students will encounter 3-letter blends with consonant digraphs. To begin the lesson, review the difference between 3-letter blends and blends with digraphs (also known as trigraphs).

Compare the words below.

| 3-letter consonant blends | consonant trigraphs |
|---|---|
| splash | shrimp |
| strap | thrash |
| squash | shrug |

Ask students to think about the differences between the two sets of words. After listening to their responses, point out that the second set of words have both a consonant and a consonant digraph that work together as a blend. The digraph still maintains its own sound.

You might want to point out that in the letter pattern in *squa* and *qua*, the vowel makes a short *o* sound. This is because /w/ sounds like *qu* have an unusual effect on vowels. They often make vowels sound like short *o*.

## Finger Tapping

| split | 5 taps | s-p-l-i-t |
| scrub | 5 taps | s-c-r-u-b |
| squash | 4 taps | s-qu-a-sh |

## Elkonin Boxes

Model how to write the following words in Elkonin boxes.

| s | t | r | u | m |
|---|---|---|---|---|

| th | r | a | sh |
|----|---|---|----|

Next, instruct your students to use blank Elkonin boxes to write the following words:

| | |
|---|---|
| squid | sprig |
| throb | splat |
| squish | strap |

## Concept-Picture Connection

Guide Word(s): splash, shrub

## Multisensory Connections

| | | |
|---|---|---|
| split | sprig | shrill |
| throb | squish | squid |
| strap | strum | |

## Sight Words

Create index cards and practice arm tapping for the following words: *from, who,* and *as.*

# Initial 3-Letter Blends

**Read each word below.**

## Real Words

| splash | throb | sprat | shrug |
|---|---|---|---|
| scrub | strum | split | splat |
| scrap | squat | squish | thrill |

## Nonsense Words

| scrat | sprab | splin |
|---|---|---|
| thrun | shrid | shrog |

**Read each sentence below. Circle each 3-letter blend and trigraph.**

1. To see the squid was a thrill.
2. She will scrub and splash the dog in the bath.
3. The strap on the black bag had split.
4. Grab the sprig from the shrub.

**Read the decodable story. Underline the blends.**

Fin will go sled on the hill. The sled will slip. The sled will spin. The sled will go down the hill! Splat! The sled will crash—what a thrill! Fin is glad to have a sled. He will let Ron have a go on his sled. Ron will like the sled.

# Initial Blends Review

**Fill in the initial blends. Then, read the sentences and fill in the blanks.**

*Note*: The sentences contain sight words.

imp          ock

ub          ash

**1.** Did you set the _____?

**2.** I can make a _____ in the bath!

**3.** Look! I see a _____

# Lesson 3 | Final Blends

*Review*

## Introduce the New Concept

Today, students will learn to pronounce words that have final blends. As a reminder, reiterate the difference between consonant digraphs and blends.

Compare the words below.

| final consonant blends | initial and final blends |
|:---:|:---:|
| tilt | clasp |
| act | blend |
| help | trust |
| went | scalp |

The blends *-ld*, *-nk*, *-rd*, and *-rk* are covered in later lessons in greater depth since the vowel is influenced by the blend.

## Finger Tapping

| | | |
|:---:|:---:|:---:|
| kelp | 4 taps | k-e-l-p |
| slept | 5 taps | s-l-e-p-t |
| thrust | 5 taps | th-r-u-s-t |
| plump | 5 taps | p-l-u-m-p |

## Elkonin Boxes

Model how to write the following words in Elkonin boxes.

| qu | e | s | t |
|:---:|:---:|:---:|:---:|

| c | r | a | f | t |
|:---:|:---:|:---:|:---:|:---:|

Next, instruct your students to use blank Elkonin boxes to write the following words:

| | | |
|:---:|:---:|:---:|
| gasp | shift | end |
| craft | belt | held |

## Concept-Picture Connection

Guide Word(s): mask

## Multisensory Connections

| | | | |
|---|---|---|---|
| hunt | mask | lump | task |
| last | west | act | held |

## Sight Words

Create index cards and practice arm tapping for the following words: *her*, *an*, and *his*.

## Mini Assessment

Have your students spell the following words: *elf, gasp, limp,* and *trust*.

# Final Blends

**Read each word below.**

### Real Words

| | | |
|---|---|---|
| pond | gift | milk |
| nest | tent | limp |
| mask | blimp | bend |
| slept | wisp | crust |

### Nonsense Words

| | | |
|---|---|---|
| mond | selk | ment |
| belf | stelm | dilp |

**Read each sentence below.**

1. Chad and Jon did a fast craft.

2. Is her frog lost?

3. His desk is just a mess.

**Fill in the missing words.**

1. The _____ will help him act.

2. An egg will _____ if you drop it.

3. Do not jump on the _____ .

# Final Blends Mini Assessment

**Read the following words:**

| | | |
|---|---|---|
| stunt | crept | lisp |
| milk | shelf | kilt |
| weld | crimp | stump |
| clasp | fact | gulp |

**Spelling: Try your best to spell each word you hear.**

1. _____

2. _____

3. _____

4. _____

# Spelling Rule | -*ct* Ending

*Review*

## Introduce the New Concept

As a reminder, spelling rules are short lessons that are typically covered in one or two days. Encourage your students to copy down the following spelling rule in their Orton-Gillingham notebooks.

**-*ct* Rule:** If there is a /kt/ sound at the end of a word it is spelled with a -*ct*. Words are never spelled with a -*kt* ending.

## Elkonin Boxes

Model how to write the following words in Elkonin boxes.

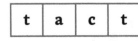 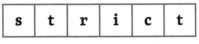

Next, instruct your students to use blank Elkonin boxes to write the following words:

| | | |
|---|---|---|
| fact | sect | act |

## Concept-Picture Connection

Guide Word(s): collect

## Multisensory Connections

| | | |
|---|---|---|
| pact | duct | tract |
| tact | act | strict |

# Spelling Rule  -*ch/-tch*

## *Review*

### Introduce the New Concept

Spelling rules are short lessons that are typically covered in one to two days. Instruct students to copy down the following new spelling rule in their Orton-Gillingham notebooks.

**-*ch/-tch*:** If a word ends in the /ch/ sound, use -*tch* if it follows a short vowel. Use -*ch* if it comes after a long vowel or consonant.

Even though students have not yet learned long vowels, they can still be introduced to the concept. At this point, they should not be expected to spell words with long vowels.

### Elkonin Boxes

Model how to write the following words in Elkonin boxes.

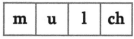

| m | u | l | ch |

| m | a | tch |

Next, instruct your students to use blank Elkonin boxes to write the following words:

bench                    fetch                    scratch

### Concept-Picture Connection

Guide Word(s): beach, catch, lunch

### Multisensory Connections

stitch                brunch                lunch

notch                itch                bench

# -*ct*, -*ch*, & -*tch* Reading Practice

**Read each word below.**

### -*ct* Real Words

| | | |
|---|---|---|
| sect | pact | tact |
| fact | duct | strict |

### -*ct* Nonsense Words

| | |
|---|---|
| flict | vuct |
| muct | fect |

### -*ch*/-*tch* Real Words

| | | |
|---|---|---|
| bunch | notch | brunch |
| stench | bench | stitch |
| match | munch | lunch |
| itch | batch | latch |

### -*ch*/-*tch* Nonsense Words

| | |
|---|---|
| pench | vulch |
| kitch | gitch |

**Read the following decodable sentences and underline the -*ct*/-*ch*/-*tch* words.**

1. First, we can sit on the bench, then we can make a pact.

2. Did you smell the stench? I have a hunch that it is the fish.

3. My cat can act like a dog when I tell him to fetch.

## Lesson 4 | Glued Sounds -*am* & -*an*

*Review*

## Introduce the New Concept

A glued sound is a letter pattern that is glued together. This means that while one can hear the sounds in the pattern, they are hard to separate when decoding the word. For this reason, it is best to teach glued sounds as a pattern rather than as individual sounds. The words below contain an /am/ or /an/. When these letters are together, they make a nasal sound. To reinforce this, instruct students to plug their noses while saying a few words with the glued patterns. They will notice that the sound comes out of their noses rather than their mouths.

Review the words below:

| -*am* | -*an* |
|-------|-------|
| ham | pan |
| scram | plan |
| Pam | sand |
| slam | man |

## Finger Tapping

| | | |
|------|--------|----------|
| ram | 2 taps | r-am |
| scan | 3 taps | s-c-an |
| ban | 2 taps | b-an |
| scram | 4 taps | s-c-r-am |
| yam | 2 taps | y-am |

## Elkonin Boxes

Model how to write the following words in Elkonin boxes. Glued sounds share a box in Elkonin boxes.

Next, instruct your students to use blank Elkonin boxes to write the following words:

| | | |
|------|------|------|
| Sam | gram | ham |
| can | clan | tram |

## Concept-Picture Connection

Guide Word(s): jam, pan

## Multisensory Connections

| | | |
|---|---|---|
| tan | span | clam |
| ran | bam | Sam |
| ham | Stan | |

## Sight Words

Create index cards and practice arm tapping for the following words: *for, if,* and *your*.

Name: _____ Date: _____

# Glued Sounds - *am* & - *an*

**Write the word depicted in the illustration underneath each picture.**

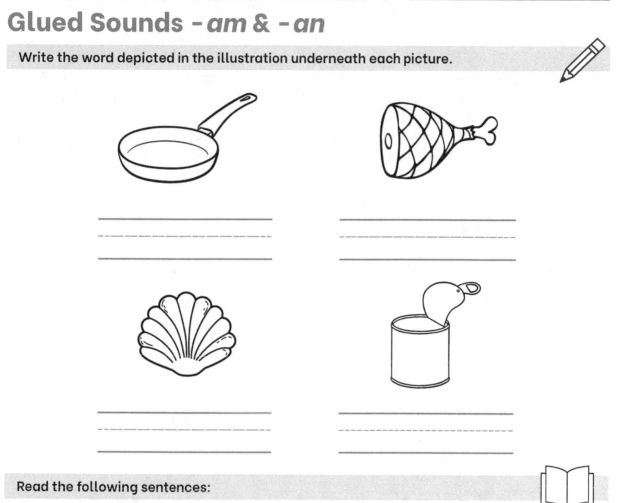

_____

_____

_____

_____

**Read the following sentences:**

1. Do you see the clam in the sand?
2. What is the grand plan?
3. Do not pet the ram with your hand.
4. Can you grab the plant from the van?
5. The tram can pick us up.

**Read the decodable story. Circle any words with - *am* or - *an*.**

Sam is a ram. Sam is a ram with lots of fluff. He has a pal. His pal is Pam. Pam is a clam with a big shell. Pam and Sam like to be by the sand. Pam will swim. Ram will run on the sand and get wet. Pam and Sam like to have fun.

## Lesson 5 | Glued Sounds *-al* & *-all*

*Review*

### Introduce the New Concept

As mentioned in the previous lesson, a glued sound is a letter pattern that is glued together. This means that while one can hear the sounds in the pattern, they are hard to separate while decoding the word. In the glued sound /all/, the *a* does not make a typical short /a/ sound (as one would expect since it is closed in by the *ll*). Instead, the *a* takes on the sound of short *o*. Remind your students that words ending with *-all* have a double *l* because they follow the doubling rule taught in Unit 1 (see page 89).

This also applies to single-syllable words with *-al*. Point out this vowel sound discrepancy as you review the words below. Two of the words listed under the *-al* section are not yet decodable so don't expect your students to read or spell them independently at this point. But, it is helpful to point them out now so they see that the /l/ influences the sound of the vowel.

| *-all* | *-al* | typical short /a/ |
|--------|-------|-------------------|
| ball | malt | bat |
| call | salt | mad |
| stall | chalk | cab |
| mall | walk | snack |

Perceptive students may notice that words with an *-oll* typically make a long /o/ sound as in toll, droll, and knoll. This is not taught explicitly because this pattern accounts for very few words. An exception to this is the word doll.

### Finger Tapping

| call | 2 taps | c-all |
|------|--------|-------|
| hall | 2 taps | h-all |
| small | 3 taps | s-m-all |
| salt | 3 taps | s-al-t |
| stall | 3 taps | s-t-all |

## Elkonin Boxes

Model how to write the following words in Elkonin boxes. Glued sounds share a box in Elkonin boxes.

| h | al | t |
|---|----|---|

| s | m | all |
|---|---|-----|

Next, instruct your students to use blank Elkonin boxes to write the following words:

|        |        |
|--------|--------|
| fall   | salt   |
| tall   | call   |
| all    | malt   |

## Concept-Picture Connection

Guide Word(s): ball

## Multisensory Connections

|        |        |
|--------|--------|
| call   | stall  |
| tall   | mall   |
| halt   | malt   |
| small  | wall   |

## Sight Words

Create index cards and practice arm tapping for the following words: *that*, *are*, and *use*.

## Mini Assessment

Ask students to spell the following words: *malt*, *all*, *small*, and *tall*.

# Glued Sounds -*al* & -*all*

**Read each word below.**

## Real Words

| tall | squall | stall |
|------|--------|-------|
| gall | ball | fall |
| small | hall | wall |
| salt | mall | halt |

## Nonsense Words

| trall | grall |
|-------|-------|
| zalt | palt |

**Read the following sentences and then underline any words that contain -*al* or -*all*.**

1. Can I go to the mall for the salt?

2. Pam had a fall in the hall.

3. Halt! Is that a pig in the stall?

**Read the sentences below and then fill in the blanks.**

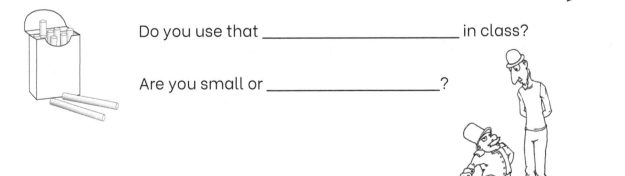

Do you use that _____ in class?

Are you small or _____?

Name: _____     Date: _____

# Glued Sounds Mini Assessment #1

**Read the following words:**

| clamp | gall | mulch |
|-------|-------|-------|
| talk | strict | grand |
| rich | duct | wall |
| stand | patch | stitch |

**Spelling: Try your best to spell each word you hear.**

1. _____

2. _____

3. _____

4. _____

# Lesson 6 | Glued Sound -*ng*

*Review*

## Introduce the New Concept

This lesson is the first introduction to silent letters. The glued sound -*ng* can be paired with *a, i, o,* and *u*. When the -*ng* is next to a vowel sound, the vowel is slightly different. It is helpful to point out that the tongue sticks to the roof of the mouth when making the /-ng/ (and /-nk/) sound. Emphasize that the -*g* in this pattern is silent. It is there to influence the sound of the vowel and the *n*.

| **ang** | **ing** | **ong** | **ung** |
|---------|---------|---------|---------|
| rang    | king    | long    | hung    |
| sang    | bring   | gong    | lung    |

## Finger Tapping

| | | |
|--------|--------|----------|
| fang   | 2 taps | f-ang    |
| hung   | 2 taps | h-ung    |
| fling  | 3 taps | f-l-ing  |
| thing  | 2 taps | th-ing   |
| strong | 4 taps | s-t-r-ong |

## Elkonin Boxes

Model how to write the following words in Elkonin boxes. Glued sounds share a box in Elkonin boxes.

Next, instruct your students to use blank Elkonin boxes to write the following words:

| | | |
|------|------|-------|
| bang | tong | bring |
| ring | dung | pang  |

## Concept-Picture Connection

Guide Word(s): king, gong, lung, bang

## Multisensory Connections

| | |
|---|---|
| wing | gong |
| song | tang |
| lung | ring |
| fling | hung |

## Sight Words

Create index cards and practice arm tapping for the following words: *him, there,* and *has.*

# Glued Sound-*ng*

**Read each word below.**

### Real Words

| | | |
|---|---|---|
| fling | rang | sang |
| pong | bring | thing |
| sung | hung | sang |

### Nonsense Words

| | |
|---|---|
| hing | jang |
| plong | trung |

**Read the sentences below and underline any words that end in -*ng*.**

1. The bell will ring.
2. She has to bring the pan to the king.
3. There is a bat with fangs in the hut.
4. Can you bang the gong?

**Read the story below and then underline any words that end in -*ng*.**

Two bats are in the hut. You can call the first bat Ling. Ling has small fangs. Ling has a pal. His pal is Cam. Cam will sing. Ling will flap his wings. Cam and Ling will make a fast dash in the hut. Ling and Cam are pals.

**Circle the pictures that share the same -*ng* sound.**

# Lesson 7 | Glued Sound -*nk*

*Review*

## Introduce the New Concept

The glued sound -*nk* can be paired with *a*, *i*, *o*, and *u*. When the -*nk* is next to a vowel sound, the vowel is slightly different. When making the /-nk/ sound, the tongue sticks to the roof of the mouth and then it drops to release a burst of air with the /k/ sound.

| *ank* | *ink* | *onk* | *unk* |
|-------|-------|-------|-------|
| sank | link | bonk | funk |
| bank | stink | honk | bunk |

## Finger Tapping

| | | |
|---|---|---|
| slink | 3 taps | s-l-ink |
| chunk | 2 taps | ch-unk |
| rank | 2 taps | r-ank |
| think | 2 taps | th-ink |
| bonk | 2 taps | b-onk |

## Elkonin Boxes

Model how to write the following words in Elkonin boxes. Glued sounds share a box in Elkonin boxes.

Next, instruct your students to use blank Elkonin boxes to write the following words:

| | | |
|---|---|---|
| clonk | pink | mink |
| junk | tank | bunk |

## Concept-Picture Connection

Guide Word(s): rink, honk, bunk, sank

## Multisensory Connections

| | | |
|---|---|---|
| wing | fling | ring |
| song | gong | hung |
| lung | tang | sing |

## Sight Words

Create index cards and practice arm tapping for the following words: *sit*, *been*, and *many*.

## Mini Assessment

Ask students to spell the following words: *stink*, *bonk*, *blank*, and *dunk*.

# Glued Sound -*nk*

**Read each word below.**

## Real Words

| | | |
|---|---|---|
| link | hunk | thank |
| honk | sank | chunk |
| sunk | think | blink |
| rank | bonk | funk |

## Nonsense Words

| | |
|---|---|
| sonk | mank |
| hink | bronk |
| glunk | vink |

**Read the following sentence and then circle any -*nk* words.**

1. Have you been to the rink?
2. The skunk did stink!
3. Sit down and have a pink drink.
4. The junk is in the tank.
5. How many slam dunks can you make?

**Write the -*nk* word illustrated by each picture below and then write your own rhyming word!**

1. _____    _____

2. _____    _____

3. _____    _____

# Glued Sounds Mini Assessment #2

**Read the following words:**

|         |         |         |
|---------|---------|---------|
| sink    | bunk    | sank    |
| rink    | tank    | chunk   |
| conk    | honk    | brink   |

**Spelling: Try your best to spell each word you hear.**

1. _____

2. _____

3. _____

4. _____

# Unit 2 Post-Test

**Read each word below.**

| | | |
|---|---|---|
| flap | snatch | mall |
| grill | thank | tram |
| flub | rung | tract |
| ran | long | rasp |
| malt | whisk | flinch |

**Read the sentences below.**

1. Grab the bench and the tall drum.
2. Come sing a song for us.
3. I ran fast. Sam did not catch up.
4. We can see if the tank tops match.

**Try your best to spell the words of the pictures below.**

**Circle the pictures that rhyme.**

# Unit 3: Closed Syllables

## Tips, Tricks, and Things to Know

This unit introduces students to multisyllabic words with closed syllables along with two spelling rules: closed syllable exceptions and the 1 • 1 • 1 rule.

### Finger Tapping Syllables

Multisyllabic words are tapped one syllable at a time. As noted in previous units, each tap represents one sound. As a refresher, consonant digraphs and sounds like *-ck, ss, ff, ll,* and *zz,* are all one tap because they make one sound. Glued sounds such as *-an, -am, -all, -ng,* and *-nk* also get one tap because the sounds cannot be separated easily.

We prefer to have students tap the syllable, and then lightly pound their fist at the end of the syllable. You may choose to do this with your students. Once students begin learning syllabication rules, you will likely notice that they do not need to finger tap as often. Eventually "scooping" syllables will suffice for many students. For an example of scooping, see the picture on page 13.

Here are some examples:

| | | |
|---|---|---|
| bathtub | 6 taps | b-a-th(pound) t-u-b(pound) |
| cactus | 6 taps | c-a-c(pound) t-u-s(pound) |
| rabbit | 6 taps | r-a-b(pound) b-i-t(pound) |
| cabin | 5 taps | c-a-b(pound) i-n(pound) |

### Finger Tapping Closed Syllable Exceptions

The closed syllable exceptions, *old, ost, olt, ind,* and *-ild,* are tapped the same way as glued sounds, with three fingers "glued" together.

Here are some examples:

| | | |
|---|---|---|
| scold | 3 taps | s-c-old |
| finding | 3 taps | f-ind(pound) ing(pound) |

## Using Elkonin Boxes with Multisyllabic Words

By now your students should be fairly proficient with using Elkonin Boxes to break up sounds. You may now begin using Elkonin Boxes to break up syllables. If students need more practice with breaking down sound, you may choose to break the Elkonin boxes further.

| Compound Words: Divide Between Base Words | |
|---|---|
| sun | tan |
| **Closed Syllable: VC/CV** | |
| hid | den |
| in | dex |
| **Closed Syllable: VC/V** | |
| cab | in |

## Syllabication Rules

1. All syllables have one vowel sound.
2. Compound words should be divided between the two base words.
3. If two consonants appear in between two vowels, divide them in half.
4. If three consonants appear between two vowels, determine which two belong together. Blends and digraphs should not be separated.
5. When one consonant is in-between two vowels, first try dividing after the consonant to keep the vowel closed in. If that doesn't sound right, try dividing before the consonant to keep the vowel open.
6. Never divide a vowel team or diphthong in half.
7. If there are two vowels in the middle of a multisyllabic word that *do not* work as a team, divide them in half.
8. The syllable type consonant *-le* pattern is its own syllable and should be divided as one.

## Steps for Dividing Syllables

1. First, locate the vowel or the vowel sounds in the word. Write V underneath.

2. Then, look between the vowels. Label the letters in between. Use the following codes:

   - C for consonant
   - C digraph or Cd for consonant digraph
   - C blend or Cb for consonant blend
     You might want to tell your students to put little lines under each letter in a blend or a digraph with a big line underneath. It reminds students that although there are two letters, digraphs make only one sound.

3. Draw a line between the two syllables. Remember, you cannot divide a digraph or a blend. If there are two possible blends such as in in the word "hundred," usually the second blend stays together.

4. Remember, these syllables are all closed, so your line will always appear after a consonant. If it was after the vowel, that would signal that the vowel is long and open. This skill is taught in Unit 6.

## Spelling Rules

**Closed Syllable Exceptions:** If a word has the pattern *-old*, *-ost*, *-olt*, *-ind*, or *-ild*, the vowel is long.

*Exceptions*: *-ost* and *-ind* can be short or long such as in the words cost, lost, and wind.

**The 1•1•1 Rule:** If a one-syllable word ends in one vowel followed by one consonant, you must double the consonant when adding a vowel suffix such as in *ing*, *ed*, or *est*.

*Exceptions*: Do not double the consonant in words ending with *-w*, *-x*, or *-y* such as in taxed, flowing, and staying.

## Guide Words

Guide words are a visual representation that highlight the taught skill. Use these words when referring to a specific skill. By the end of the unit, students will have a total of 13 Concept-Word Connection Cards with these guide words. These cards teach students about patterns rather than learn about a sound. When they review the cards, have them say the pattern followed by the guide word. For example, for the compound-word card, they would say, "compound word, shell-fish."

These are the guide words used in the lesson:

1. Compound Words: shellfish
2. Closed Syllables VCCV, VCCCV: cactus, rabbit, pumpkin, anthem
3. Closed Syllables VCV: lemon, rocket
4. Closed Syllable Exceptions: child, find, mold, colt, host

The 1•1•1 Spelling Rule: hop-hopping

## Sight Words

Here are the sight words covered in this unit: *each, made, were, find, now, some, long, way, part, they, time, would, about, oil,* and *these.*

## Optional Materials for Extension

To introduce the concept of dividing syllables, you may want to use cocktail straws, Play-Doh, or modeling clay to create a line to place between syllables. Or, you may want to instruct students to cut the index cards to indicate the placement of the syllable division. The cut cards make it easy to play sorting or memory games.

# Unit 3 Pretest

**Draw a line to divide these words into syllables and then read each word.**

| | | |
|---|---|---|
| pinball | basket | habit |
| muffin | salad | childish |

**Read the following words:**

| | | |
|---|---|---|
| suntan | backdrop | rocket |
| wagon | attic | method |
| mild | anthem | tunnel |
| rotten | laptop | binding |

**Read the following sentences:**

1. The colt will drink from the dish.

2. You can backtrack your steps to find your backpack.

3. The kitten will go wild for the catnip.

4. Bring your tennis racket for the match.

**Spell the words of each of the pictured items below.**

_____          _____

# Practice Literacy at Home

Dear Parents/Guardians,

Today we begin Unit 3: Closed Syllables. Closed syllables have one vowel sound and they end with a consonant. For example, the one-syllable word, cat, has a short *a* vowel sound and it ends with the consonant *t* so it is closed. For compound words with closed syllables, we divide between the two base words, such as in cat/nip. If two consonants appear between two vowels, we divide them in half, such as in cac/tus. If three consonants appear between two vowels, we determine which two belong together. Blends and digraphs should not be separated, such as in rock/et and hun/dred. Lastly, your child will be working on the 1•1•1 spelling rule. This is when a one-syllable word ends in one vowel followed by one consonant. In such cases, you must double the consonant when adding a vowel suffix such as *ing*, *ed*, or *est*. The only exceptions are words ending with *-x*, *-w*, or *-y*, such as in taxed, flowing, and staying. The consonants in those words do not double.

If you'd like your child to practice this unit at home, here are the dates for each lesson and some words to practice reading, writing, and spelling.

| Dates: | | | | | |
|---|---|---|---|---|---|
| Skills: | Compound Words | VCCV/VCCCV Words | VC/V Words | Closed Syllable Exceptions | 1•1•1 Spelling Rule |
| Examples: | sandbox | rabbit | lemon | cold | popping |
| | bathtub | anthem | racket | post | smallest |
| | suntan | dentist | relish | child | grinning |
| | cobweb | goblet | dragon | bolt | thinnest |
| | lapdog | problem | topic | mind | hugging |

To make reading and writing even more fun, have your child use Play-Doh or colored markers or pencils to spell each word. They can even pick some of the words to draw and label!

Happy learning!

## Lesson 1 | Compound Words

*Review and Pretest*

### Introduce the New Concept

This lesson is the first introduction to multisyllabic words. Today, students will learn to separate compound words between their two base words.

Before showing students how to separate words, review the syllabication rules on page 131. Since we will be focusing on the first two rules today, ask your students to copy those rules into the Notes section of their Orton-Gillingham notebook:

1. All syllables have one vowel sound.

2. Compound words should be divided between the two base words.

Next, take a few moments to brainstorm about compound words. Make a list of compound words on index cards and then demonstrate how to separate the syllables using Play-Doh, clay, straws, scissors, or a marker. Here are some index card ideas:

|           |          |          |
|-----------|----------|----------|
| catnip    | bathtub  | upend    |
| zigzag    | cannot   | dishcloth |

### Finger Tapping

| pinball  | 5 taps | p-i-n(pound) b-all(pound)    |
| setup    | 5 taps | s-e-t(pound) u-p(pound)      |
| bellman  | 5 taps | b-e-ll(pound) m-an(pound)    |
| shellfish | 6 taps | sh-e-ll(pound) f-i-sh(pound) |

### Elkonin Boxes

To place multisyllabic words into Elkonin Boxes, put each syllable in one box. If students need additional scaffolding, you may choose to break down the boxes further.

Next, instruct your students to use blank Elkonin boxes to write the following words:

|          |          |
|----------|----------|
| nutshell | sunset   |
| tiptop   | laptop   |

## Concept-Picture Connection

Guide Word(s): shellfish

## Multisensory Connections

| | |
|---|---|
| hotrod | bathmat |
| tomcat | pigpen |
| catnip | uphill |

## Sight Words

Create index cards and practice arm tapping for the following words: *each*, *made*, and *were*.

# Compound Words

Draw a line to split each word into syllables and then read each word.

| | | |
|---|---|---|
| dishpan | tomcat | tiptop |
| lapdog | pigpen | suntan |
| upset | pinball | sunset |
| bathmat | hatbox | uphill |
| catfish | cobweb | bathtub |

Read each sentence. Circle the compound words.

1. Glen made the tomcat upset.
2. Will each of you go uphill for the sunset?
3. Does the hotrod go fast?
4. The catnip made the cats yell.
5. The lapdog looks like a puffball.
6. Your room is like a pigpen. It is a big mess!
7. Can you have the shellfish?

Use the pictures to make a compound word.

 +  = _____

  = _____

# Lesson 2 | Closed Syllables VCCV & VCCCV

*Review*

## Introduce the New Concept

Today, students learn to separate multisyllabic words with the VCCV and VCCCV patterns. They will be working with closed syllables only.

Before showing students how to separate words with the VCCV or VCCCV pattern, review the syllabication rules on page 131. Tell your students to copy the third and fourth rules into the Notes section of their Orton-Gillingham notebook (we will also be covering the first rule today but that one has already been recorded into their notebooks):

3. If two consonants appear in between two vowels, divide them in half.

4. If three consonants appear between two vowels, determine which two belong together. Blends and digraphs should not be separated.

Make a list of VCCV and VCCCV words on index cards and then model how to separate them using Play-Doh, clay, straws, scissors, or simply a marker. Here are some index card ideas:

cactus (simple VC/CV split)  pumpkin (VC blend/CV split)

rabbit (double letter VC/CV split)  anthem (VC/C digraph V split)

## Finger Tapping

| | | |
|---|---|---|
| sandal | 5 taps | s-an(pound) d-a-l(pound) |
| gossip | 6 taps | g-o-s(pound) s-i-p(pound) |
| fragment | 8 taps | f-r-a-g(pound) m-e-n-t(pound) |
| anthem | 4 taps | an(pound) th-e-m(pound) |
| disrupt | 7 taps | d-i-s(pound) r-u-p-t(pound) |

## Elkonin Boxes

To place multisyllabic words into Elkonin Boxes, put each syllable in one box. If students need additional scaffolding, you may want to break down the boxes further.

| mag | net |
|---|---|

| hid | den |
|---|---|

Next, instruct your students to use blank Elkonin boxes to write the following words:

lentil

puppet

goblet

enchant

hundred

skillet

## Concept-Picture Connection

Guide Word(s): cactus, rabbit, pumpkin, anthem

## Multisensory Connections

lesson

problem

enlist

happen

basket

chopstick

## Sight Words

Create index cards and practice arm tapping for the following words: *find, now, some,* and *long.*

## Mini Assessment

Ask students to spell the following words: *rabbit, basket, kitten,* and *subtract.*

# Closed Syllables VCCV & VCCCV

**Read each word below.**

## Real Words

| | | |
|---|---|---|
| muffin | signal | conduct |
| tennis | children | contest |
| goblet | selfish | sunlit |

## Nonsense Words

| | |
|---|---|
| vonnect | fobbit |
| flimflap | slithpan |

**Read each sentence. Split the syllables if you need help.**

1. Can you find some baskets?
2. Now can we go to the pigpen?
3. The contest is at sunset.
4. I have a muffin for lunch.
5. The skillet is red hot!
6. Do you have one hundred cats?
7. The rabbit will hop to the shed.

**Read each sentence and then fill in the blank with the words illustrated in the pictures.**

Did you see the _____?

Bring the _____ for lunch.

# Closed Syllables
# Mini Assessment

**Read the following words:**

| | |
|---|---|
| falcon | uplift |
| disgust | campus |
| suspect | impress |
| cosmic | sluggish |
| extend | random |

**Spelling: Try your best to spell each word you hear.**

1. _____

2. _____

3. _____

4. _____

# Lesson 3 | Closed Syllables VC/V

*Review*

## Introduce the New Concept

Today, students learn to separate multisyllabic words with the VC/V pattern. They will be working with closed syllables only.

Before showing students how to separate words with the VCV pattern, review the syllabication rules on page 131. Today's lesson focuses on the first and fifth rules. Ask students to copy the fifth rule into the Notes section of their Orton-Gillingham notebook where they copied the first four rules during the first two lessons of this unit:

5.  When one consonant is in-between two vowels, first try dividing after the consonant to keep the vowel closed in. If that doesn't sound right, try dividing before the consonant to keep the vowel open.

Make a list of words on index cards and then demonstrate how to separate them using Play-Doh, clay, straws, scissors, or a marker. Here are some index card ideas:

lemon (simple VC/V split)

rocket (VC digraph/V split)

wagon (VC/V split with schwa)

method (VC digraph/V split)

## Schwa

Students may notice that the /o/ in wagon sounds more like an *uh*. Sometimes, the letters *a, u, i,* and *o* sound more like a short /u/ or /i/ sound. This unexpected vowel sound is called schwa. It happens in words with an unstressed syllable. Typically, students do not have trouble reading words with this sound, but they may have trouble spelling them. Spelling words with an unstressed syllable is often a matter of memorization. Students may begin to recognize patterns where the schwa sound is common. To help them recognize such patterns, point out words with similar endings, such as comma and gamma. At this point, it is too early to expect students to spell words with the schwa sound correctly all of the time. But, point out the schwa sound so students become familiar recognizing it.

## Finger Tapping

| | | |
|---|---|---|
| topic | 5 taps | t-o-p(pound) i-c(pound) |
| ticket | 5 taps | t-i-ck(pound) e-t(pound) |
| gravel | 6 taps | g-r-a-v(pound) e-l(pound) |
| relish | 5 taps | r-e-l(pound) i-sh(pound) |
| dragon | 6 taps | d-r-a-g(pound) o-n(pound) |

## Elkonin Boxes

To place multisyllabic words into Elkonin Boxes, put each syllable in one box. If students need additional scaffolding, you may want to break down the boxes further.

| sev | en |
|---|---|

| com | et |
|---|---|

Next, instruct your students to use blank Elkonin boxes to write the following words:

| | | |
|---|---|---|
| gallon | melon | solid |
| clinic | chapel | gravel |

## Concept-Picture Connection

Guide Word(s): lemon, rocket

## Multisensory Connections

| | | |
|---|---|---|
| ticket | gravel | solid |
| dozen | model | habit |

## Sight Words

Create index cards and practice arm tapping for the following words: *way*, *part*, *they*, and *time*.

# Closed Syllables VC/V

**Read each word below.**

| | | |
|---|---|---|
| finish | visit | bucket |
| lemon | novel | closet |
| salad | limit | wagon |
| topic | denim | devil |

**Read each sentence. Split the syllables if you need help.**

1. Did you like the long novel?
2. Is this part of the lemon?
3. I have a ticket to see the talent.
4. Which way is the dragon den?
5. Can you tell me the topic?
6. Is that my denim jacket?
7. This method is the best way to do the job.

**Cut out the syllables below. Glue them together to make two words. Then, write the words on the line.**

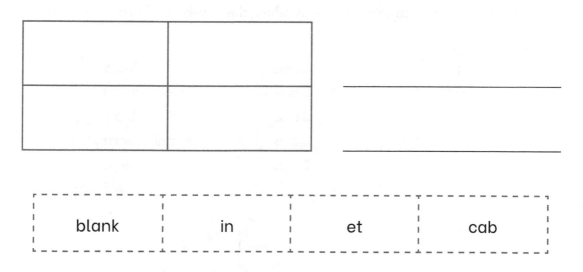

| | |
|---|---|
| | |
| | |

_____

_____

| blank | in | et | cab |

# Lesson 4 | Closed Syllable Exceptions

*Review*

## Introduce the New Concept

Today's lesson covers a new spelling rule. Unlike other spelling rules, this one will be a full lesson since it is the first introduction to long vowel sounds. Instruct students to copy down the following spelling rule in their Orton-Gillingham notebooks.

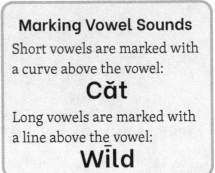

**Marking Vowel Sounds**

Short vowels are marked with a curve above the vowel:

## Că̆t

Long vowels are marked with a line above the vowel:

## Wīld

If a word has the pattern *old, ost, olt, ind,* or *-ild*, the vowel is long.

> *Exceptions*: *-ost* and *-ind* can be short or long as in the words cost, lost, and wind.

Explain that in these syllables, the vowels make their long sound, or "say their names." For example, in *-ild* and *ind*, we hear the /i/ saying its long sound rather than its short sound.

In *old, ost,* and *olt*, we hear the /o/ in its long sound versus short sound format. To emphasize the difference, mark the vowels with either a straight line for long vowel sounds, or a curved line for short vowel sounds. Although we hear the long sound in words with these patterns, such words are exceptions to the rule. In any other closed syllables, the vowels are short.

## Finger Tapping

| | | |
|---|---|---|
| hold | 2 taps | h-old |
| most | 2 taps | m-ost |
| bolt | 2 taps | b-olt |
| binding | 3 taps | b-ind(pound) ing(pound) |
| mild | 2 taps | m-ild |

## Elkonin Boxes

Model how to write the following words in Elkonin boxes.

| s | c | old |
|---|---|-----|

| b | ind |
|---|-----|

Next, instruct your students to use blank Elkonin boxes to write the following words:

| | |
|---|---|
| mild | rind |
| post | bold |
| bolt | kind |

## Concept-Picture Connection

Guide Word(s): child, find, mold, colt, host

## Multisensory Connections

| | | |
|---|---|---|
| wild | most | mind |
| cold | bolt | mild |

## Sight Words

Create index cards and practice arm tapping for the following words: *would*, *about*, *oil*, and *these*.

Name: _____  Date: _____

# Closed Syllable Exceptions

**Read each word below.**

| | | |
|---|---|---|
| cold | molt | bold |
| wild | grind | colt |
| fold | blind | find |
| most | host | childish |
| kind | mild | bolting |
| jolt | post | folding |

**Read each sentence.**

1. Would you like to hop on the gold swing?
2. What time will the host have us?
3. It is a mild spring day.
4. They will scold the child.
5. Can you find the block?
6. The rind is still on the lemon.

**Read the passage and then answer the questions below.**

### The Gold Colt

One spring day, a child was walking on a path next to a ranch. He saw a pig and a chicken. When he went to pet the pig in its pigpen, the pig said to him, "I am Hamlet and I do not wish to be pet." *What a shock! The pig can talk?*

In a panic, the child went to pet the chicken. The chicken said to him, "I am Cluck and I wish to be pet! I have a bad itch on my chin." *The chicken can talk?* With a small scratch, the chicken was glad.

The child had to ask, "How can you two talk?" Hamlet told him that a small colt with locks of gold put a spell on them. Hamlet and Cluck were children from a distant ranch. They told the child they saw the gold colt one day. The glint of the gold locks was so vivid, they felt they had to pet him! They did, but the colt did not like that and scolded them. With just a wink, they were now a pig and a chicken. The child said to Hamlet and Cluck, "I will find the colt. He can fix this!"

He left to find him. It was not long until he saw him by a post. The child went to the colt. The colt did not look wild, but kind and sad. The child went to pet his gold locks, but first he said, May I pet you?" The colt said, "Yes, but can you pull out this small twig? A part of it is stuck in my shin." *Yank!* The child did pull the twig from his shin. "Now it is out. Can you help my buds Hamlet and Cluck?" the child said to the colt?" The kind colt said, "Yes," and they went to them. With a quick wink, the two went back to who they were! The colt told them that they can pet him, but first they must ask!

**1.** How was the spell put on Hamlet and Cluck?

_____

_____

_____

_____

**2.** Did the colt like to be pet? What did the colt tell Hamlet and Cluck must happen first?

_____

_____

_____

_____

# Spelling Rule | 1•1•1 Rule

*Review*

## Introduce the New Concept

As a reminder, spelling rules are short lessons that are typically covered in one or two days. Instruct students to copy down the following spelling rule in their Orton-Gillingham notebooks.

**The 1•1•1 Rule:** If a one-syllable word ends in one vowel followed by one consonant, you must double the consonant when adding a vowel suffix such as *ing*, *ed*, or *est*.

*Exceptions*: Don't double the consonant in words ending with *-x*, *-w*, or *-y*, as in taxed, flowing, and staying.

## Elkonin Boxes

Model how to write the following words in Elkonin boxes. The examples are broken into syllables, but you may want to break the boxes down further if your students need additional support.

| hop | ping |
|-----|------|

| plan | ning |
|------|------|

Next, instruct your students to use blank Elkonin boxes to write the following words:

biggest                    running                    wedded

## Concept-Picture Connection

Guide Word(s): hop-hopping

## Multisensory Connections

patting                    reddish

shopping                   camping

tallest                    chatted

# 1·1·1 Spelling Rule

**Read each word below.**

| | | |
|---|---|---|
| thinnest | hosted | batted |
| twisting | sniffing | messing |
| dripping | madness | rubbing |
| hugging | admitted | |

**Read the following sentences:**

1. Smelling the muffins from the kitchen is one way to tell when the time is almost up.

2. He is grabbing his lunchbox first, then he is stopping by.

3. Sam handed Ron the pack of folded bathmats.

4. Finn is planning to bring relish for the hotdogs.

5. I will grab the smallest pen, so it will fit in my pocket.

**Combine the word and its ending. Write the new word on the line.**

1. upset + ing = _____

2. post + ed = _____

3. swim + ing = _____

4. rub + ish = _____

5. pop + ing = _____

6. fit + ed = _____

# Unit 3 Post-Test

**Draw a line to divide these words into syllables, then read each word.**

| catfish | pigpen | golden |
|---------|--------|--------|
| disgust | packet | finish |

**Read each word below.**

| cannot | uplift | closet |
|--------|--------|--------|
| planet | topic | colt |
| child | mothball | rabbit |
| kitten | dentist | finding |

**Read the sentences below.**

1. Bring the bucket for the milk.
2. Did you find your laptop? Put it in your backpack.
3. Are you singing a song for the talent contest?
4. Bring your tennis balls to the match.

**Spell the words illustrated in each picture below.**

_____      _____

# Unit 4: Silent *E*

## Tips, Tricks, and Things to Know

This unit introduces students to long vowels in words with a silent *e* pattern, along with two spelling rules, *-ive* and the *e*-drop rule.

### Finger-Tapping Syllables

At this point in the text, finger tapping is no longer as necessary as it was in earlier units. But, if you feel that your students still need intensive decoding work, encourage them to continue to finger tap. When tapping a word with the silent *e* pattern, only tap sounds that can be heard.

At this point, most students will make the transition to dividing words into syllables rather than tapping each sound. Here is an example of finger tapping within a silent *e* word:

| | | |
|---|---|---|
| stake | 4 taps | s-t-a-ke |

### Using Elkonin Boxes with Silent e

Here is how to use Elkonin boxes to break up words with the silent *e* pattern. As a reminder, the silent *e* does not get its own box since the sound is not heard. Instead, it goes in the box with the sound preceding it.

| s | l | i | de |
|---|---|---|----|
| m | a | ke | |
| th | e | se | |

### Dividing Syllables with Silent e

The same syllabication and labeling rules reviewed in Unit 3 apply when using a silent *e*, with one additional factor. When breaking up multisyllabic words with a silent *e*, the silent *e* is not separated from its influenced vowel. To demonstrate, ask students to label the silent *e* with a star and then draw an arrow from the silent *e* to the vowel it is making long. If the silent *e* is in the first syllable, the word is divided right after it.

## Spelling Rules

**The -*ive* Exception:** When a word ends in -*ive*, the vowel can be short or long. A few examples include give, chive, expensive, and live.

**The *e*-Drop Rule:** When a word ends in silent *e*, drop the *e* before adding a vowel suffix such as *ing*, *ed*, *er*, or *est*. Keep it if the suffix begins with a consonant such as *ly*, *ment*, or *ty*.

*Exceptions*: The *e* is not dropped in words ending with -*ee*, -*oe*, or -*ye* as in seeing, hoed, or dyeing. It is also not dropped in the words acreage, mileage, and singeing.

## Guide Words

Guide words are a visual representation that highlight the taught skill. Use these words when referring to a specific skill. By the end of the unit, students will have a total of 12 Concept-Word Connection Cards with these guide words. Have your students say the vowel pattern followed by the guide word when they review the cards. For example, for the *aCe* card, they would say, "silent *e*, cake, *a*." These are the guide words used in the lesson:

1. *aCe*: cake
2. *iCe*, *oCe*: kite, cone
3. *eCe*, *uCe*: here, cube, tune
4. Multisyllabic Magic *e*: reptile, pinecone, valentine

Spelling Rule -*ive* Exception: live, live

Spelling Rule *e*-Drop Rule: bite-biting, tasted

## Sight Words

Here are the sight words covered in this unit: *could, into, call, other, word, write, their, water, number, people, over, new, sound, take, only, little, work,* and *know*.

## Optional Materials for Extension

One of our favorite things to do with our students is to make a magic *e* wand. We make a big deal of getting out the art supplies to decorate a wand with an *e* pasted at the top of it. Then we use the *e* to hold up to words with a short vowel to make them long.

# Unit 4 Pretest

**Read the words below.**

| | | |
|---|---|---|
| cake | lede | hike |
| twine | fade | dote |
| Pete | role | dude |
| mute | grade | mine |

**Draw a line to divide these words into syllables.**

| | | |
|---|---|---|
| pancake | bonfire | clambake |
| pollute | upside | pinecone |

**Read the sentences below.**

1. Who is your valentine?
2. Look at the tall flames from the campfire!

3. Come see the cute kitten sitting in the sunshine.
4. Did Mr. Pete give you a note or a grade on your test?

**Spell the words illustrated in the pictures.**

_____     _____

# Practice Literacy at Home

Dear Parents/Guardians,

Unit 4: Silent *E* introduces the long vowel sounds. These words contain a long vowel sound and end with the letter e. We call this a magic *e* because it has magic powers that makes the vowel "say its name." Examples of magic *e* words are listed below. Remember *C* stands for consonant. The -*ive* exception is when a word ends in -*ive*. In those cases, the vowel can be short or long, such as in give, chive, expensive, or live. The *e*-Drop Rule is when a word ends in silent *e*, drop the *e* before adding a vowel suffix such as -*ing*, -*ed*, -*er*, or -*est*. But we keep it if the suffix begins with a consonant such as -*ly*, -*ment*, or -*ty*. There are, however, a few exceptions. For example, the *e* is not dropped in words ending with -*ee*, -*oe*, or -*ye* as in seeing, hoed, or dyeing. It is also not dropped in the words acreage, mileage, and singeing.

If you'd like your child to practice this unit at home, here are the dates for each lesson and some words your child can practice reading, writing, and spelling.

| Dates: | | | | | | |
|---|---|---|---|---|---|---|
| Skills: | *aCe* | *iCe, oCe* | *uCe, eCe* | Multisyllabic Silent *e* | -*ive* Exception | *e*-Drop Rule |
| Examples: | brake | pole | rule | bagpipe | drive | hoping |
| | rate | note | cube | concave | thrive | giving |
| | lake | fire | theme | handshake | festive | shaded |
| | made | site | eve | valentine | give | wasting |
| | fade | mite | mule | upgrade | outlive | closing |
| | stale | stone | flute | mixtape | | |

To make reading and writing even more fun, have your child use Play-Doh or colored markers or pencils to spell each word. They can even pick some of the words to draw and label!

Happy learning!

# Lesson 1 | Magic *e: aCe*

## *Review and Pretest*

### Introduce the New Concept

Today, students will learn a new spelling pattern, silent *e*. Begin by reviewing the short sounds of the vowels. Next, explain that this new pattern makes the vowels say their other sound. This sound is referred to as a long sound. Another way to explain it is by saying that silent *e* has magic powers. As such, it is often referred to as magic *e*. Magic *e* has the power to jump over consonants (usually just one) to make the preceding vowel in the word "say its name." Next, review the following short vowel to long vowel examples.

| short *a* | *aCe* |
|:---:|:---:|
| rat | rate |
| Sam | same |
| mad | made |
| slat | slate |

There are a few words that have more than one consonant between the vowel and the silent *e*. A couple of examples include waste and bathe. You may choose to cover these now, or as they come up. As always, students should go with the most common sound pattern first and then work their way through other options if necessary.

### Finger Tapping

| make | 3 taps | m-a-ke |
|:---:|:---:|:---:|
| slate | 4 taps | s-l-a-te |

### Elkonin Boxes

To place silent *e* words into Elkonin boxes, put the silent *e* in the same box as the consonant preceding it.

Next, instruct your students to use blank Elkonin boxes to write the following words:

| snake | cave | same |
|:---:|:---:|:---:|
| mane | gave | brake |

## Concept-Picture Connection

Guide Word(s): cake

## Multisensory Connections

| | | |
|---|---|---|
| date | fate | tame |
| cane | vase | gale |

## Sight Words

Create index cards and practice arm tapping for the following words: *could, into,* and *call.*

# Magic *e*: *aCe*

## Read each word below.

| | | |
|---|---|---|
| cape | blame | pane |
| grape | shave | date |
| Kate | ate | grave |
| chase | whale | sake |

## Read each sentence. Underline the magic *e* words.

1. I wish I could bake the cake, but I am at the lake.
2. Walk into the glade and you will see the snake.
3. Can you call me if you see the whale at the cape?
4. The kids rave about her grape cake.
5. Is that the same cape?
6. The big insect was a small lunch for the snake.
7. Is your pet tame or wild?
8. Will you bring your cane on the plane?
9. The gale wind is strong.
10. Does Kate have a date for brunch?

## Use the pictures below to make a long *a* plus magic *e* word.

# Lesson 2 | Magic e: iCe & oCe

*Review*

## Introduce the New Concept

Today, students continue to learn about reading and spelling words with the magic *e* pattern. Begin by reviewing short vowel sounds. Then introduce words with a long *i* and a long *o*. Review the words below.

| short *i* | *iCe* |
|:---:|:---:|
| pin | pine |
| kit | kit |

| short *o* | *oCe* |
|:---:|:---:|
| con | cone |
| tot | tote |

## Finger Tapping

| slide | 4 taps | s-l-i-de |
|:---:|:---:|:---:|
| hone | 3 taps | h-o-ne |

## Elkonin Boxes

To place silent *e* words into Elkonin boxes, put the silent *e* in the same box as the consonant preceding it.

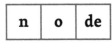  

Next, instruct your students to use blank Elkonin boxes to write the following words:

| | |
|:---:|:---:|
| ripe | dime |
| hope | rope |
| ride | note |

## Concept-Picture Connection

Guide Word(s): kite, cone

## Multisensory Connections

| | |
|---|---|
| tote | pine |
| bite | hide |
| cone | lobe |
| cope | pipe |

## Sight Words

Create index cards and practice arm tapping for the following words: *other*, *word*, and *write*.

## Mini Assessment

Ask students to spell the following words: *fine, poke, gate,* and *make.*

# Magic *e*: Long *i* & *o* Words

**Read each word below.**

### Real Words

| | | |
|---|---|---|
| cope | rose | pride |
| chime | cove | twine |
| mite | ride | zone |
| wove | hope | tine |

### Nonsense Words

| | |
|---|---|
| dite | chipe |
| lote | bire |

**Read each sentence. Underline the magic *e* words.**

1. Can you write my name on the kite?
2. Her bike is at home.
3. I hope you have a ride to the cove.
4. Will you write the word on the line?
5. Do not hit the spike or you will pop your bike tire.
6. Clide is at the job site.
7. The spice made the salad bad.
8. Will you give that dog the bone? He will not bite.
9. She wove the blanket for me.
10. I need to doze off and then I will go home.

**Use the pictures to make long *o* and *i*, magic *e* words.**

 +  (e) = _____

+ (e) = _____

# Magic *e*: Long *a*, *i*, & *o* Words
# Mini Assessment

**Read the following words:**

| | | |
|---|---|---|
| mite | stone | rote |
| lake | time | shame |
| spoke | gave | blame |
| shine | cone | pile |

**Spelling: Try your best to spell each word you hear.**

1. _____

2. _____

3. _____

4. _____

# Lesson 3 | Magic e: eCe & uCe

*Review*

## Introduce the New Concept

Today, we will continue reading and spelling words with the magic *e* pattern. Begin by reviewing the short vowel sounds. Next, explain that you will be covering words with a long *e* and a long *u*. Review the words below.

| short *e* | eCe |
|-----------|-----|
| them | theme |
| pet | Pete |

| short *u* | uCe |
|-----------|-----|
| mut | mute |
| tub | tube |

The long *u* can actually make two sounds. As an example, explain that in the word mute, we hear a distinct long *u* sound, but in the word tube, we hear an /oo/. Until students are more comfortable with these sounds, encourage them to make both long *u* sounds while they attempt to decode unfamiliar words.

## Finger Tapping

| fluke | 4 taps | f-l-u-ke |
|-------|--------|----------|
| mere | 3 taps | m-e-re |

## Elkonin Boxes

To place silent *e* words into Elkonin boxes, put the silent *e* in the same box as the consonant preceding it.

| h | e | re |
|---|---|----|

| J | u | ne |
|---|---|----|

Next, instruct your students to use blank Elkonin boxes to write the following words:

| cute | Eve |
|------|-----|
| theme | rule |
| dude | Crete |

## Concept-Picture Connection

Guide Word(s): here, cube, tune

## Multisensory Connections

| | | |
|---|---|---|
| fuse | these | plume |
| crude | here | fluke |

## Sight Words

Create index cards and practice arm tapping for the following words: *their, over, new, water, number,* and *people.*

# Magic *e*: *eCe* & *uCe*

**Read each word.**

## Real Words

| | | |
|---|---|---|
| theme | rude | mule |
| rule | flume | fuse |
| fluke | mere | crude |
| here | plume | lede |

## Nonsense Words

| | |
|---|---|
| dume | mebe |
| chule | tepe |

**Read each sentence. Underline the magic *e* words.**

1. We need to stick to the rule.
2. Five is the mere number of people I expect to come.
3. The water flume ride is so much fun!
4. I am here at the theme park.
5. If I eat a prune I will puke.
6. The flute is from Crete.
7. Will Eve and Pete be here in June?
8. Will you use the plume to write the note?
9. The mule is not over here.
10. Can you fix the fuse?

**Use the pictures to make magic *e* words.**

+ e = _____

+ e = _____

# Lesson 4 | Multisyllabic Silent *e*

*Review*

## Introduce the New Concept

Today, students will continue reading and spelling multisyllabic words with the magic *e* pattern. Begin by reviewing each vowel's short and long sounds. Then explain that students will learn to read and spell multisyllabic words with the silent *e* pattern. Emphasize that when dividing syllables in a word with the silent *e* pattern, the silent *e* must stay with the vowel it is influencing. Otherwise, the same syllabication rules that were taught in Unit 3 should be followed.

Make a list of words on index cards and then demonstrate how to separate them using Play-Doh, clay, straws, scissors, or a marker. Ask students to star the magic *e* and draw an arrow to the vowel that it is influencing. Here are some index card ideas:

|  |  |
|---|---|
| vampire | pancake |
| basement | sunshine |

## Finger Tapping

| bonfire | 6 taps | b-o-n(pound) f-i-re(pound) |
|---|---|---|
| sideswipe | 7 taps | s-i-de(pound) s-w-i-pe(pound) |

## Elkonin Boxes

To place multisyllabic silent *e* words into Elkonin boxes, put each syllable in its own box.

| ig | nite |
|---|---|

| home | made |
|---|---|

Next, instruct your students to use blank Elkonin boxes to write the following words:

| milestone | reptile | windpipe |
|---|---|---|
| lifelike | sandstone | wildfire |

## Concept-Picture Connection

Guide Word(s): reptile, pinecone, valentine

## Multisensory Connections

| sidekick | trombone | rosebud |
|---|---|---|
| pavement | update | cupcake |

## Sight Words

Create index cards and practice arm tapping for the following words: *only*, *little*, *work*, *sound*, *take*, and *know*.

# Magic *e*: Multisyllabic Silent *e*

**Read each word below.**

### Real Words

| | | |
|---|---|---|
| athlete | upgrade | inflate |
| sunrise | explode | basement |
| umpire | concave | sidekick |
| mistake | complete | upsize |

### Nonsense Words

| | |
|---|---|
| flipflame | dockpote |
| dingmone | injole |

**Read each sentence and underline the magic *e* words.**

1. The little rosebush is next to the grass.

2. Pete will work on a fix for the mistake.

3. She did not know how to play the bagpipes.

4. There is only one umpire at the baseball game.

5. I dislike the red snakeskin bag.

6. The fast tadpole will try to escape from the net.

7. Ted would like to subscribe to the list.

8. There is a dispute over the man's land.

9. Can you divide the muffin for me?

10. Will you run up the slope at an incline?

**Read the story and then answer the questions.**

### The New Broth

It was a cold day. Jamal and Kate were sitting by the fire. Jamal's mom came out with a classic broth drink for the kids.

Jamal said, "Yum Mom, thank you!" Kate was not as kind. She said, "Yuck! What is that? I do not like that kind of broth. At my home, we do not have that. I do not want to sip on that!" Then she said, "I only like my mom's broth. I will not have that disgusting drink!"

This made Jamal sad. The broth his mom made was something he had pride in. His mom spent a lot of time chopping carrots, radishes, and kale to make it. They used nutmeg and salt to make it the best it could be. Jamal spent time helping her mix up the broth. Kate did not take one sip. With one look, she said she did not like it.

When Kate's mom came to pick her up from Jamal's home, she said, "What is that good smell?" Jamal's mom said, "That is my broth. Kate did not want to taste it, but you are welcome to have a mug full!" Kate's mom had one sip and said, MMMMM, that is so rich!" Kate felt shame. She could have a sip.

Kate put the mug to her lips and had a small sip. "Yum!" she said. "That is quite divine, Jamal!" Kate had been rude, and she must make it up to Jamal and his mom. She said, "Jamal, it was rude of me to not sip your mom's broth. I feel shame for my attitude. I made a mistake. I will aspire to give new things a go." Jamal did smile and Kate said thank you for the broth.

**1.** What did Kate do when she got the broth?

_____

_____

_____

_____

**2.** Do you think Kate was acting rude when she did not sip the broth? What makes you think this?

_____

_____

_____

_____

# Spelling Rule | -ive Exception
### *Review*

## Introduce the New Concept

As a reminder, spelling rules are short lessons that are typically covered in one or two days. Instruct students to copy down the following spelling rule in their Orton-Gillingham notebooks.

**-*ive* Exception:** When a word ends in -*ive*, the vowel can be short or long.

The reason that -*ive* can be short or long is because the letter *v* can never be at the end of a word. At times, the *e* is there to keep the *v* company, but other times it is there to make the *i* long. Encourage students to use context clues to determine which way to pronounce words with this pattern (for example, "I live in the city" or "that is a live snake).

## Elkonin Boxes

Model how to write the following words in Elkonin boxes.

| h | i | ve |
|---|---|----|

| pas | sive |
|-----|------|

Next, instruct your students to use blank Elkonin boxes to write the following words:

give                    thrive                    five

## Concept-Picture Connection

Guide Word(s): live (long), live (short)

## Multisensory Connections

festive                drive                outlive

massive                strive                pensive

## Spelling Rule | *e*-Drop Rule

*Review*

### Introduce the New Concept

Today, we will cover another spelling rule. Have students review the meaning of a base word prior to starting this lesson. Then, instruct them to copy down the following spelling rule in their Orton-Gillingham notebooks.

**e-Drop Rule:** When a word ends in silent *e*, drop the *e* before adding a vowel suffix such as *ing*, *ed*, *er*, and *est*. Keep the *e* if the suffix begins with a consonant such as *ly*, *ment*, and *ty*.

Show students a few examples of the suffix being added to the base word, such as those noted below:

hope + *ing* = hoping

joke + *ing* = joking

waste + *ed* = wasted

Words with -*ed* endings are reviewed again in Unit 6.

### Concept-Picture Connection

Guide Word(s): bite-biting, tasted

### Multisensory Connections

|  |  |
|---|---|
| traded | smiling |
| wasting | shaking |
| fading | diving |

# -*ive* Exception and the *e*-Drop Rule

**Read each word below.**

## -*ive* Words

| | | |
|---|---|---|
| captive | chive | passive |
| active | festive | thrive |
| olive | live (long) | dive |
| hive | live (short) | give |

### *e*-Drop Words

| | | |
|---|---|---|
| hope-hoping | scrape-scraping | smoke-smoking |
| bite-biting | taste-tasted | save-saving |
| chose-chose | use-useless | close-closing |

**Combine the word and its ending. Write the new word on the line.**

1. grade + *ing* = _____

2. use + *ing* = _____

3. waste + *ed* = _____

4. shade + *ed* = _____

5. skate + *ing* = _____

# Unit 4 Post-Test

**Try your best to read these words.**

| | | |
|---|---|---|
| skate | chive | inline |
| flute | mane | muted |
| theme | flaking | noting |
| dole | restive | active |

**Draw a line to divide these words into syllables and then read the words.**

| | | |
|---|---|---|
| upside | fireman | console |
| commute | grateful | incomplete |

**Read these sentences. Underline the magic *e* words.**

1. Do not mope or whine, I am driving your dog home.

2. Look at the smoke! The campfire is too big!

3. Will you visit Crete when you take your trip?

4. To make the base for the model dome, we must first put the tubes into the cubes.

**Spell the words illustrated in the pictures below.**

_____        _____

# Unit 5: Vowel Teams

## Tips, Tricks, and Things to Know

This unit introduces students to long vowels in words that exhibit a regular vowel team pattern.

### Finger Tapping Syllables

At this point in the text, most students have made the transition to chunking words into syllables rather than tapping out each sound. Each lesson in this unit includes a few examples of finger tapping to reinforce the concept, but feel free to skip this section if you feel it is unnecessary.

If your students still require the support of finger tapping, here are examples of finger tapping within a vowel team word:

| | | |
|---|---|---|
| team | 3 taps | t-ea-m |
| groan | 4 taps | g-r-oa-n |

### Using Elkonin Boxes with Vowel Teams

Here is how to use Elkonin boxes to break up words with the vowel team pattern. All vowel teams share a box since they make one sound.

In this unit and each unit thereafter, students will begin phasing out the use of Elkonin box practice. Teachers should model how to break the words into boxes. If students need additional practice, they can use any of the practice words in the lesson.

| f | r | ai | l |
|---|---|----|---|

| t | r | ee |
|---|---|----|

| t | oe |
|---|----|

## Dividing Syllables with Vowel Teams

Remind your students that the syllabication and labeling rules covered in previous units still apply, with one exception.

The only additional factor to breaking up multisyllabic words with vowel teams is that vowel teams should not be separated. Encourage students to label the vowel team by underlining both letters in the team and using the label VT to remind them to keep the letters together.

## Spelling Rules

Consider reviewing previously taught spelling rules during the review portion of your lessons since there are no new spelling rules to introduce in this unit.

## Guide Words

Guide words are a visual representation that highlight the taught skill. Use these words when referring to a specific skill. By the end of the unit, students will have a total of 10 Concept-Word Connection Cards featuring these guide words. When they review the cards, tell them to say the vowel pattern followed by the guide word. For example, for the *ea* card, they would say, "*ea*, beach, long /e/." These are the guide words used in the lesson:

1. *ea*, *ee*: beach, tree
2. *ai*, *ay*: snail, play
3. *oa*, *oe*: boat, toe
4. *ue*, *ui*, *ie*: rescue, clue, fruit, pie

## Sight Words

Here are the sight words covered in this unit: *place*, *year*, *live*, *me*, *back*, *give*, *most*, *very*, *after*, *things*, *our*, *just*, *name*, *good*, *sentence*, *man*, *think*, *say*, *great*, and *where*.

## Homophones

Several of the lessons in this unit include homophones that relate to the spelling patterns. You may want to extend the learning process by practicing these words. See page 15 for more information about homophones, homographs, and homonyms.

Name: _____  Date: _____

# Unit 5 Pretest

**Read the words below.**

| | | |
|---|---|---|
| tray | meat | fruit |
| toe | pain | display |
| oat | true | mistreat |
| feel | tie | explain |

**Read the sentences below.**

1. On Sunday we can take the boat to the lake.

2. I need to find a coat that will match my suit.

3. I cannot wait to eat the homemade pie.

4. You may stay home, but first you must clean the flue.

5. Put the roe next to the fruit tray.

**Spell the words illustrated in the pictures below.**

p _____ l

gl _____

m _____ l

t _____

TEACH READING with **Orton-Gillingham**

# Practice Literacy at Home

Dear Parents/Guardians,

Today, we start our journey into Unit 5: Vowel Teams. By now, your child has learned the rhyme, "When two vowels go walking, the first one does the talking." This unit introduces students to the vowel teams *ea/ee* (long *e* sound), *ai/ay* (long *a* sound), *oa/oe* (long *o* sound), *ie* (long *i* sound), and *ue/ui* (long *u* sound). When spelling words with these sounds there are a few tricks to learn. For the vowel patterns *ai/ay*, *ai* occurs at the beginning or middle of words and syllables, while *ay* is always at the end. For the vowel patterns *oa/oe*, the *oa* occurs at the beginning or middle of words and syllables, while *oe* is always at the end. The vowel pattern *ui* occurs in the middle of words and syllables, while *ue* is usually at the end. The *ie* pattern is not common and is always found at the end of words. Your child will also be learning about homophones, which are words that sound the same but are spelled differently, such as meet and meat. Homophones can be difficult to learn and usually require repetitive practice through reading and spelling.

If you'd like your child to practice this unit at home, here are the dates for each lesson and some words your child can practice reading, writing, and spelling. Words in parentheses are homophones.

| Dates: | | | | |
|---|---|---|---|---|
| Skills: | Sound of *e*: *ea*, *ee* | Sound of *a*: *ai*, *ay* | Sound of *o*: *oa*, *oe* | Sound of *u* and *i*: *ue*, *ui*, and *ie* |
| Examples: | tea (tee) | braid | coat | glue |
| | sleep | ray | toe | fruit |
| | feet (feat) | pain | road (rode) | pie |
| | sweet | stray | doe | clue |
| | meat (meet) | bait | oak | suit |
| | bleach | crayon | aloe | tie |

To make reading and writing even more fun, have your child use Play-Doh or colored markers or pencils to spell each word. They can even pick some of the words to draw and label or write a story.

Happy learning!

# Lesson 1 | Vowel Teams *ea & ee*

## *Review and Pretest*

## Introduce the New Concept

Today's unit covers regular vowel teams, the most common type of vowel team. At this point in the text, students have mastered two other syllable types—closed and silent *e*.

To begin the lesson, introduce your students to this rhyme, "When two vowels go walking, the first one does the talking." Explain that this rhyme will not always ring true, but for the purpose of learning about regular vowel teams, it is a great memory tool.

Explain that you will cover two vowel teams in this lesson, *ea* and *ee*. Both of these vowel teams make the long *e* sound. Students now know three patterns that make a long *e*: *eCe*, *ee*, and *ea*.

Create a chart showing words that fall under each pattern.

| *eCe* | *ea* | *ee* |
|---|---|---|
| theme | team | bee |
| Eve | clean | feet |
| these | flea | wheel |

## Finger Tapping

| peach | 3 taps | p-ea-ch |
|---|---|---|
| sweep | 4 taps | s-w-ee-p |

## Elkonin Boxes

To place words with regular vowel teams into Elkonin boxes, put each vowel team in its own box.

| s | l | ee | p |
|---|---|---|---|

| s | p | ea | k |
|---|---|---|---|

## Concept-Picture Connection

Guide Word(s): beach, tree

## Multisensory Connections

| peep | teach | teeth |
|---|---|---|
| clean | three | teak |

## Sight Words

Create index cards and practice arm tapping the following words: *place, year, live, me,* and *back*.

## Homophones

See How to Use This Book on page 15 for more details.

| | | |
|---|---|---|
| team-teem | tee-tea | peek-peak |
| beat-beet | sea-see | week-weak |

# Vowel Teams *ea* & *ee*

**Read each word below.**

## Real Words

| | | | |
|---|---|---|---|
| least | beat | three | bleed |
| cream | beet | seat | creep |
| wheel | reap | jean | dream |

## Nonsense Words

| | |
|---|---|
| sneech | speen |
| veat | skeel |

**Read each sentence. Underline the *ea/ee* words.**

1. Will you meet me at the beach or at Pete's place?

2. I live in the home by the creek.

3. Last year I swam near the reef.

4. The water is deep and clean.

5. Can you hand me a red beet?

6. Please heed my call when you hear it.

7. Did that dog have fleas?

8. I will teach you how to make tea.

9. The seal needs to eat the fish.

10. The child made a squeal of glee when he saw the treat.

**Fill in each blank with either *ea* or *ee* to spell a real word.**

p _____ ch                   str _____ t

tr _____                     b _____ ns

sh _____ p                   l _____ f

m _____ n                    t _____ th

# Lesson 2 | Vowel Teams *ai* & *ay*

*Review*

## Introduce the New Concept

Today's lesson introduces a second set of vowel teams, the sounds of long *a*. As a reminder, review the rhyme, "When two vowels go walking, the first one does the talking."

Introduce the two new vowel teams for this lesson, *ai* and *ay*. Both of these vowel teams make the long *a* sound. Students now know three patterns that make a long *a*: *aCe*, *ai*, and *ay*.

The vowel pattern *ai* occurs at the beginning or middle of words while *ay* is always at the end of a word or syllable. Use a chart to show some words that fall under each pattern.

| *aCe* | *ai* | *ay* |
|-------|------|------|
| cake | snail | play |
| base | mail | may |
| shame | trail | clay |

## Finger Tapping

| rail | 3 taps | r-ai-l |
|------|--------|--------|
| say | 2 taps | s-ay |

## Elkonin Boxes

To place words with regular vowel teams into Elkonin boxes, put each vowel team in its own box.

| t | ai | l |
|---|----|----|

| t | r | ay |
|---|---|----|

## Concept-Picture Connection

Guide Word(s): snail, play

## Multisensory Connections

| drain | faint | may |
|-------|-------|-----|
| jay | bray | aid |

## Sight Words

Create index cards and practice arm tapping for the following words: *give, most, very, after,* and *things.*

## Homophones

| | | |
|---|---|---|
| mail-male | plain-plane | waist-waste |
| maid-made | tail-tale | main-mane |

## Mini Assessment

Ask students to spell the following words: *drain*, *leap*, *feel*, and *spray*.

# Vowel Teams *ai & ay*

**Read each word below.**

## Real Words

| | | |
|---|---|---|
| spray | slay | pay |
| faith | strain | frail |
| main | vain | sail |
| raid | day | stay |

## Nonsense Words

| | |
|---|---|
| glay | slail |
| cail | thray |

**Read each sentence. Underline the *ai/ay* words.**

1. Please give me back my clay tray.
2. I want to lay by the bay today.
3. Did you hear the dog bray? It is on the trail of a skunk!
4. There is a very small stain on the waist of your dress.
5. Most of the time, she has a braid in her hair.
6. Is that a snail in your pail, or just a shell?
7. "You are just a ray of sunshine today!" my mom said.
8. Can the stray dog stay with you? We need to find him a home.
9. Is that fuzz stuck in the drain?
10. Will you hike the trail in May?

**Circle the correct word illustrated in each picture.**

rayn   rain

play   plai

tray   trai

brayd   braid

clay   clai

trayn   train

Name: _____  Date: _____

# Vowel Teams
# Mini Assessment

**Read the following words:**

| | |
|---|---|
| chain | tea |
| sway | display |
| beat | spleen |
| meet | Spain |
| slain | reach |

**Spelling: Try your best to spell each word you hear.**

1. _____

2. _____

3. _____

4. _____

# Lesson 3 | Vowel Teams *oa* & *oe*

*Review*

## Introduce the New Concept

Today's lesson focuses on the sounds of long *o*. As a reminder, review the rhyme, "When two vowels go walking, the first one does the talking."

Explain that you will cover two vowel teams in this lesson, *oa* and *oe*. Both of these vowel teams make the long *o* sound. Students now know three patterns that make a long *o*: *oCe*, *oa*, and *oe*.

The vowel pattern *oa* occurs at the beginning or middle of words while *oe* is always at the end. Use a chart to show words that fall under each pattern.

| oCe | oa | oe |
|---|---|---|
| tote | gloat | toe |
| poke | soap | foe |
| close | toast | doe |

## Finger Tapping

| foam | 3 taps | f-oa-m |
|---|---|---|
| hoe | 2 taps | h-oe |

## Elkonin Boxes

| b | oa | t |
|---|---|---|

| f | oe |
|---|---|

To place words with regular vowel teams into Elkonin boxes, put each vowel team in its own box.

## Concept-Picture Connection

Guide Word(s): boat, toe

## Multisensory Connections

| toast | boat |
|---|---|
| Moe | float |
| roast | toe |

## Sight Words

Create index cards and practice arm tapping for the following words: *our, just, name, good,* and *sentence.*

## Homophones

road-rode                    soar-sore                    boar-bore

Name: _____  Date: _____

# Vowel Teams *oa* & *oe*

**Read each word below.**

### Real Words

| Joe | bloat | doe |
| oat | soak | coast |
| hoe | soap | coach |

### Nonsense Words

| noak | voat |
| koe | ploat |

**Read each sentence. Underline the *oa/oe* words.**

1. Let's load the truck with the soap.
2. Is your throat sore? You sound hoarse.
3. Joe and Moe will go to the coast after they finish here.
4. Your oat loaf is the best!
5. "Just go to Joe's after swim lessons," Mom said.
6. Is your coat too hot for the boat ride?
7. Which things will you bring on your trip to Joan's house on the coast?
8. Our coach can loan you a ball for the game.
9. I will hoe the plot of land to plant pumpkins.
10. Can I soak the cups in the soap?

**Write the correct word illustrated in each picture.**

toes or toas? _____

goat or goet? _____

toed or toad? _____

aloe or aloa? _____

# Lesson 4 | Vowel Teams *ue, ui,* & *ie*

## Review

## Introduce the New Concept

Today we will work on the sounds of long *u* and long *i*. The long *u* actually makes two sounds. In some cases, the long *u* sounds like /yoo/. In other cases, it sounds like /oo/. The /oo/ sound is much more common, but both are possible. The *ui* pattern always sounds like /oo/ while the *ue* pattern can sound like /yoo/ or /oo/. Long *i* is most often represented in open syllables or silent *e* patterns, although there are some words with the *ie* vowel team pattern.

This lesson covers three vowel teams, *ue, ui,* and *ie*. This means that students now know several patterns that make long *u* and long *i*.

The vowel pattern *ui* occurs in the middle of words while *ue* is most often at the end. The less common *ie* pattern is always found at the end of words. Use a chart to show words that fall under each pattern.

| *ue* | *ui* | *ie* |
|------|------|------|
| value | suit | pie |
| blue | cruise | die |
| cue | fruit | lie |

## Finger Tapping

| hue | 2 taps | h-ue |
|------|--------|------|
| bruise | 4 taps | b-r-ui-se |

## Elkonin Boxes

| p | ie |
|---|----|

| s | ui | t |
|---|----|---|

| t | r | ue |
|---|---|----|

## Concept-Picture Connection

Guide Word(s): rescue, clue, fruit, pie

## Multisensory Connections

| clue | true | suit |
|------|------|------|
| die | fuel | vie |

## Sight Words

Create index cards and practice arm tapping for the following words: *man, think, say, great,* and *where*.

# Vowel Teams *ue*, *ui*, & *ie*

**Read each word below.**

## Real Words

| | | |
|---|---|---|
| venue | due | sue |
| cruise | pie | hue |
| rue | undue | fruit |
| tie | accrue | suit |

## Nonsense Words

| | |
|---|---|
| nuit | nie |
| fue | scue |

**Read each sentence. Underline the *ue*/*ui*/*ie* words.**

1. What is the name of the man in the blue suit and black tie?

2. Can you write a sentence about the statue?

3. Did the fruit have a bruise?

4. The man in the suit is with Sue.

5. Will the day cruise be a good venue for the lunch?

6. Can you glue the sand on that spot?

7. Find the clue and you can rescue the cat.

8. The fruit pie is a reddish hue.

9. I like the statue because it has a good hat.

10. Please help me pick the fruit for lunch.

**Read the story and then answer the questions.**

### Frog and Snail

Frog and Snail were sitting on a log in the bog. They were thinking about life in the swamp and chatting about each other's swamp homes.

Frog's home was a small oak log on the side of the swamp. It had fruit with a blue hue winding over it. The log was small but had soft moss on the inside. It was safe and kept him hot as toast when it was cold outside.

Snail, on the other hand, had made his home in a plastic boat that a small child had left in the swamp years ago. Snail's home could pass on the water as the wind went through the trees. Snail did like the sense of change. He did like the feel of the wind from the breeze as his boat floated along.

Yet, despite the fact that they had very distinct homes, both buds were glad. They did not compete over who had the best home, and they did not boast that their home was best. They realize that each animal in the swamp has a set of needs. They know that they do not have to be the same to be buds!

Frog and Snail have distinct likes and needs, but they do have a fondness for each other!

**1.** Where do Frog and Snail live?

_____

_____

**2.** Compare and contrast their homes.

_____

_____

# Unit 5 Post-Test

**Read the words below.**

| | | |
|---|---|---|
| fray | seat | suit |
| foe | stain | mainstay |
| toast | blue | boastful |
| reel | lie | swimsuit |

**Read the following sentences:**

1. The cream and coffee are for after our feast.

2. I will bring your suit and tie to the wedding.

3. We can play in the sand at Seal Beach on Sunday.

4. You will need beads and glue for this project.

5. Clean up all of the nails. I do not want to cut my toe.

**Spell the words illustrated in the pictures below.**

f _____ t

fr _____ t

p _____ l

p _____ s

# Unit 6: Open Syllables

## Tips, Tricks, and Things to Know

This unit introduces students to long vowels in words with open syllables.

### Finger Tapping Syllables

If your students still require the support of finger tapping, here are a few examples within an open syllable word:

| | | |
|---|---|---|
| try | 3 taps | t-r-y |
| hoping | 4 taps | h-o(pound) p-ing(pound) |

### Using Elkonin Boxes with Multisyllabic Open-Syllable Words

Here is how to divide words with open syllables into Elkonin boxes. If students need more practice with breaking down individual sounds, you may want to break the Elkonin boxes further.

| Open Syllables in Multisyllabic Words | |
|---|---|
| ba | by |
| li | on |

| Open Syllables in a One-Syllable Word |
|---|
| hi |

### Dividing Syllables with Open Syllables

Remind students that the same syllabication and labeling rules covered in previous units still apply. But with this lesson, they will learn a new twist.

When dividing a word with an open syllable, divide immediately after the vowel to leave it open so the vowel can "shout its name." Encourage your students to write the syllable type(s) under each syllable to assess understanding.

Your students have already been introduced to the first five Syllabication Rules on page 131. These are the remaining syllabication rules. Students have already copied rules 1–5, but will review Rule 5 during this unit.

5. When one consonant is in-between two vowels, first try dividing after the consonant to keep the vowel closed in. If that doesn't sound right, try dividing before the consonant to keep the vowel open.

6. Never divide a vowel team or diphthong in half.

7. If there are two vowels in the middle of a multisyllabic word that *do not* work as a team, divide them in half.

8. The syllable type consonant *-le* pattern is its own syllable and should be divided as one.

## Schwa

Schwa is known as a lazy vowel. It occurs in unaccented syllables and sounds like /uh/ as in amaze, Alabama, and animal. We teach it as an explicit lesson in this unit (see page 207), but it was also covered briefly in Unit 3 (see page 143), and your students have likely encountered this pattern before. It will be covered more in Unit 7 with *r*-influenced vowels (see page 215).

## Spelling Rules

**Plurals Ending in *y* Rule:** If a word ends in a vowel sound and then *y*, just add -*s*. If a word ends in a consonant and then *y*, drop the *y* and add -*ies*.

*Exceptions*: This rule does not apply to proper nouns.

**Suffix -*ed* Rule:** Suffix -*ed* can make three sounds: /d/ (moved), /ed/ (planted), and /t/ (jumped).

- Base words that end with a voiceless sound such as *p, k, s, f, ch*, soft *th*, and *sh* sound like /t/
- Base words that end with a voiced sound such as *b, g, v, j, z, l, m, n, r*, hard *th*, or long vowel sound like a /d/
- Base words that end with a *t* or *d* sound like /ed/ at the end

## Guide Words

Guide words are a visual representation that highlight the taught skill. Use these words when referring to a specific skill. By the end of the unit, students will have a total of 13 Concept-Word Connection Cards with these guide words. When they review the cards, encourage them to say the pattern followed by the guide word. For example, for the relax card, they would say, "open syllable VCV, relax." These are the guide words used in the lesson:

1. Open One-Syllable Words: cry, she
2. Open Syllables in Two-Syllable Words: baby, relax
3. V/V Syllabication: lion, poem
4. Schwa: animal, Alaska

Spelling Rule Plurals Ending in *y*: families, decays

Spelling Rule Suffix -*ed*: cleaned, planted, jumped

## Sight Words

Here are the sight words covered in this unit: *help, through, much, before, line, right, too, means, old, any, same, tell, boy, follow, came,* and *want*.

# Unit 6 Pretest

Name: _____     Date: _____

## Read the following words:

| | | |
|---|---|---|
| cries | shy | patched |
| flu | comma | client |
| jumped | babies | trial |
| fluid | filled | slyly |

## Read the following sentences:

1. Write a poem that describes your family.

2. The robotic lion looked so real.

3. The ladies walked to the front of the line quietly.

4. Do you want this on your salad? We also have pecans and tomatoes.

5. Use the atlas to find Alaska. Begin by looking west of Canada.

## Fill in the blank with the missing word or the word with its ending.

1. puppy + *s* = _____

2. _____ + *s* = bullies

3. stop + *ed* = _____

4. _____ +*ed* = clipped

# Practice Literacy at Home

Dear Parents/Guardians,

We are beginning Unit 6: Open Syllables. Open syllables are syllables that end with an open vowel (a vowel not followed by a consonant) and the vowel "says its name." For example, words like go, be, and she are all open syllables—you can hear the vowel's name in the syllable. Your child will be learning how to read these open syllables in one- and two-syllable words. Some words, like client, follow a vowel-vowel pattern (V/V). In these cases, your child will learn to split the syllable between the vowels (cli/ent). We will also be learning the schwa sound. Schwa makes the /uh/ sound, but can be spelled with different vowels like in the word banana. Lastly, your child will be learning how to add or change endings to words. First, we will review how to spell plural words that end with *y*, such as changing baby to babies and delay to delays. We will also learn how to read words with the -*ed* suffix, which can make three different ending sounds. For example, -*ed* in wanted sounds like /ed/, but -*ed* in milked sounds like /t/, and -*ed* in billed sounds like /d/.

If you would like your child to practice this unit at home, here are the dates for each lesson as well as some words your child can practice reading, writing, and spelling.

| Dates: | | | | | |
|---|---|---|---|---|---|
| Skills: | Open One-Syllable Words | Open Syllables in Two-Syllable Words | Vowel/Vowel Syllabication | Spelling Rule Plurals Ending in *y* | Spelling Rule Suffix -*ed* |
| Examples: | cry<br>go<br>he<br>me<br>no | bingo<br>donate<br>robot<br>secret<br>rotate | lion<br>diet<br>truant<br>fluent<br>violin | tries<br>baggies<br>stays<br>plays<br>bellies | cleaned<br>tried<br>babied<br>clipped<br>granted |

To make reading and writing even more fun, have your child use Play-Doh, colored markers, or pencils to spell each word. They can even pick some of the words to draw and label!

Happy learning!

# Lesson 1 | Open One-Syllable Words

## *Review and Pretest*

### Introduce the New Concept

Today students learn a new syllable type. Your class will now know four syllable types: closed, silent *e*, vowel teams, and now, open syllables. Students have already learned many of the words in today's lesson as sight words. But today they will learn why these words are also considered "rule followers." Write down the words below. Students should know all of these words if they have been following the sight word sequence of this text.

Open Syllable "Rule Followers": go, be, she

Explain that words with an open syllable have vowels that are open at the end so they are free to "shout their names" rather than make their short sounds.

Also mention that thus far *y* has been a consonant, but in today's lesson *y* is a "chameleon," based on its placement in a word. It can make its consonant sound /y/, but it can also make a long *e*, a long *i*, and even a short *i* in some words.

Use a chart to show words that fall under each pattern. Students should not be expected to read *y* = long *e* or *y* = short *i* in this lesson. The purpose of the chart is to familiarize students with possible sounds. Students are only expected to read and spell open one-syllable words in this lesson.

| *y* = long *i* | *y* = long *e* | *y* = short *i* |
|:---:|:---:|:---:|
| cry | baby | gym |
| why | happy | mystic |
| shy | scary | rhythm |

### Finger Tapping

| | | |
|:---:|:---:|:---:|
| why | 2 taps | wh-y |
| she | 2 taps | sh-e |

### Elkonin Boxes

## Concept-Picture Connection

Guide Word(s): she, cry

## Multisensory Connections

| | | |
|---|---|---|
| so | me | shy |
| by | cry | be |

## Sight Words

Create index cards and practice arm tapping for the following words: *help, through, much, before,* and *line.*

# Open One-Syllable Words

**Read each word below.**

## Real Words

| | | |
|---|---|---|
| sly | she | spry |
| go | ply | fly |
| try | dry | my |

## Nonsense Words

| | |
|---|---|
| bly | zy |
| sho | wu |

**Read the sentences and underline the open syllables.**

1. We should go to the beach before lunch.

2. Can you help me dry this suit?

3. We have lots to get done!

4. She will go through the hall and down the steps.

5. Please don't pry. You do not need to know all of that.

6. I fly on a plane to get to the cabin.

7. He is quite spry for an old man!

8. She may be shy at first, but she will try to say hi if you give her time.

9. I will look in the window to spy on my dog. I want to see what she does when I am not home!

10. Will you fry the chicken or bake it?

**Circle the words with open syllables.**

| | | |
|---|---|---|
| flu | site | cute |
| grate | | why |
| sty | these | he |

## Lesson 2 | V/CV

*Review*

### Introduce the New Concept

Today, students learn how to divide multisyllabic words with open syllables. Begin by reviewing the previously introduced syllabication rules. Then introduce the sixth rule covered in today's lesson.

To date, students are familiar with the first five rules of syllabication covered on page 131. Ask your student(s) to review rule 5 and copy rule 6 into their notebooks to begin this lesson.

5. When one consonant is in-between two vowels, first try dividing after the consonant to keep the vowel closed in. If that doesn't sound right, try dividing before the consonant to keep the vowel open.

6. Never divide a vowel team or diphthong in half.

Use a chart to show the division of words with open syllables.

| open-closed | open-open | closed-open |
|:---:|:---:|:---:|
| be/gin | he/ro | hel/lo |
| po/em | ze/ro | can/dy |
| pi/lot | la/dy | pup/py |

### Finger Tapping

| begin | 5 taps | b-e-(pound) g-i-n(pound) |
|:---:|:---:|:---:|
| lady | 4 taps | l-a(pound) d-y(pound) |

## Elkonin Boxes

| o | pen |
|---|-----|

## Concept-Picture Connection

Guide Word(s): baby, relax

## Multisensory Connections

| | | |
|---|---|---|
| bagel | menu | even |
| apex | pupil | global |

## Sight Words

Create index cards and practice arm tapping for the following words: *right, too, means, old,* and *any.*

## Mini Assessment

Ask students to spell the following words: *shy, item, soda,* and *donate.*

Name: _____     Date: _____

# Open Syllables: Two-Syllable Words

**Read each word below.**

| | | |
|---|---|---|
| behind | April | deny |
| decay | relax | demand |
| basin | rodent | final |
| halo | menu | focus |

**Read the sentences and underline the open syllables.**

1. I need help to locate the water line.

2. I would like one of the bagels too.

3. Can you hear that music? Is it from the band?

4. Please donate your old easel to the class.

5. Mo and Lilly will go to lunch at the hotel.

6. The siren will scream if there is a fire.

7. Will you give the puppy a treat?

8. "What a fun day at bingo," Grammy said with a happy smile.

9. You must keep your desk tidy and label each supply with your name.

**Spell the word illustrated in each picture. Draw a line between the syllables.**

b _____     h _____     r _____     i _____

Name: _____ Date: _____

# Open Syllables: Two-Syllable Words
# Mini Assessment

**Read the following words:**

|          |          |          |
|----------|----------|----------|
| decay    | duty     | moment   |
| spry     | try      | equal    |
| legal    | virus    | robot    |

**Spelling: Try your best to spell each word you hear.**

1. _____

2. _____

3. _____

4. _____

# Lesson 3 | V/V Syllabication

*Review*

## Introduce the New Concept

Today's lesson introduces a new pattern of syllable division, the V/V division. This pattern is less common than those previously introduced. This pattern is different from other open syllables because a vowel follows the open syllable. At first glance, students may think that the word contains a vowel team since there are two vowels next to each other. Emphasize that while there are two vowels next to each other in these patterns, they are not vowel teams. This syllabication split is uncommon, but it occurs often enough to justify introducing this concept.

Ask your students to copy rule 7.

7. If there are two vowels in the middle of a multisyllabic word that do not work as a team, divide them in half.

To break these words into syllables, follow the same steps as with previous divisions. Label the vowels and then label any consonants in between. Since these words have no consonants between the vowels, and they are not a vowel team, they are divided down the middle. Show students how to divide the words in the V/V section below. Then remind students that words with vowel teams should not be divided.

| V/V split | vowel team |
|-----------|------------|
| react | beach |
| fluid | groan |
| neon | fruit |

## Finger Tapping

| | | |
|---|---|---|
| diet | 4 taps | d-i(pound) e-t(pound) |
| create | 5 taps | c-r-e(pound) a-te(pound) |

## Elkonin Boxes

| cli | ent |
|-----|-----|

## Concept-Picture Connection

Guide Word(s): lion, poem

## Multisensory Connections

| fluent | trial | lion |
|--------|-------|------|
| quiet | eon | react |

## Sight Words

Create index cards and practice arm tapping for the following words: *same*, *tell*, and *boy*.

# V/V Syllabication

**Read each word below.**

| | | |
|---|---|---|
| diet | eon | ruin |
| duet | lion | poem |
| react | neon | truant |
| druid | trial | react |
| dial | quiet | fluid |

**Read the sentences and underline the words with V/V syllables.**

1. Did you hear the cat react to that bang? I think it is mad!

2. Tell me more about the trial this week.

3. The boss and her client are in the same lunch spot.

4. Is there any fluid in the glass or is it empty?

5. How do you think he will create the new painting?

6. Will the rain ruin the slide or can it be left out?

7. The male lion has a fluffy mane.

8. It has been eons since we last spoke! I will call you pronto!

9. Switch the dial to a new channel, please.

10. Will you read the poem to the class? You did a great job on it!

**Read and circle the words with the V/V syllables and then draw a line splitting those syllables.**

| | | |
|---|---|---|
| fluent | defiant | cupcake |
| create | | legal |
| payday | violin | duet |

## Lesson 4 | Schwa

*Review*

## Introduce the New Concept

Schwa is a concept that is related to stressed versus unstressed syllables. This concept comes in especially handy when students are learning to read poetry.

Schwa is an unstressed syllable that makes the sound /uh/. For example, when you say the word ba-nan-a, you may notice that the second syllable is stressed, or said more loudly than the other syllables. This leaves the last sound to be unstressed (schwa). The same holds true for animal and chocolate, in which the middle syllables are said very quickly. The unstressed syllables in these words are called schwa. This means we do not hear the vowel sound clearly. Some teachers refer to schwa as being a lazy vowel. To make this concept clearer, have students identify the stressed syllable in the following words. The stressed syllables are bolded.

| | | |
|---|---|---|
| **can**cel | **bot**tom | **din**osaur |
| u**pon** | em**brace** | **rib**bon |

Schwa is coded with **ə.** You may choose to have your students mark words with this syllable above vowel schwa sounds.

## Finger Tapping

away        3 taps       a(pound) w-ay(pound)

## Elkonin Boxes

| com | ma |
|---|---|

## Concept-Picture Connection

Guide Word(s): animal, Alaska

## Multisensory Connections

| | | |
|---|---|---|
| button | amaze | enemy |
| alone | across | polite |

## Sight Words

Create index cards and practice arm tapping for the following words: *follow*, *came*, and *want*.

# Schwa

**Read each word below.**

| | | |
|---|---|---|
| signal | velvet | cotton |
| denim | agape | away |
| pecan | atlas | Mona |
| tomato | salad | Alaska |

**Read the sentences and circle the words with the schwa sound.**

1. Let's sit by the pecan tree to have our lunch.

2. My gift is the one with the pink ribbon.

3. Velma and I will be at the mall until this evening.

4. Make sure to give the signal when Bella gets here.

5. The cotton dress looks great on you!

6. That pasta will be good with the fresh basil pesto.

7. She lives in a remote spot in Alaska.

8. Ana and I will be there at 1 p.m.

**Underline the schwa words. Then mark the schwa sound by putting "ə" above it.**

| | | |
|---|---|---|
| animal | travel | retake |
| medical | | alike |
| zebra | pumpkin | fluid |

# Spelling Rule | Plurals Ending in *y*

*Review*

## Introduce the New Concept

As a reminder, spelling rules are typically covered in one or two days. Instruct students to copy down the following new spelling rule in their Orton-Gillingham notebooks.

**Plurals Ending in *y*:** If a word ends in a vowel sound and then *y*, just add -*s*. If a word ends in a consonant and then *y*, drop the *y* and add -*ies*.

*Exceptions*: This rule does not apply to proper nouns.

## Elkonin Boxes

Model how to write the following words in Elkonin boxes. These words are broken into syllables, but you may choose to break the boxes down further if your students require the additional support.

| pup | py |
|-----|------|
| pup | pies |

| la | dy |
|-----|------|
| la | dies |

| de | lay |
|-----|------|
| de | lays |

## Concept-Picture Connection

Guide Word(s): families, decays

## Multisensory Connections

fly/flies          study/studies

pony/ponies       delay/delays

# Spelling Rule | Suffix -ed

*Review*

## Introduce the New Concept

Instruct students to copy down the following new spelling rule in their Orton-Gillingham notebooks.

**Suffix -ed:** Suffix -ed can make three sounds: /d/ as in moved, /ed/ as in planted, and /t/ as in jumped.

- Base words that end with a voiceless sound (*p, k, s, f, ch*, soft *th*, and *sh* followed by -*ed*) sound like /t/

- Base words that end with a voiced sound (*b, g, v, j, z, l, m, n, r*, hard *th*, or long vowel followed by -*ed*) sound like a /d/

- Base words that end with a *t* or *d* followed by -*ed* sound like /ed/ at the end

Review the sounds in the following words:

| -*ed* /ed/ | -*ed* /t/ | -*ed* /d/ |
|------------|-----------|-----------|
| wanted | milked | billed |
| molded | buffed | cleaned |
| needed | smashed | saved |
| planted | watched | seemed |

## Elkonin Boxes

Model how to write the following words in Elkonin boxes. Note that when -*ed* sounds like /ed/, it adds a syllable. When it sounds like /t/ or /d/ it does not add a syllable.

**Two Syllables**

| want | ed |
|------|-----|

**One Syllable**

| clipped |
|---------|
| saved |

## Concept-Picture Connection

Guide Word(s): cleaned, planted, jumped

## Multisensory Connections

| folded | helped | mended |
|--------|--------|--------|
| closed | attended | pushed |

# -*y* Plurals and -*ed* Suffixes

**Read each word below.**

## -*y* Plural Words

| | |
|---|---|
| pennies | ways |
| relies | galaxies |
| skies | delays |
| poppies | bullies |
| displays | fantasies |
| treaties | puppies |

## -*ed* Words

| | | |
|---|---|---|
| finished | dropped | hugged |
| dated | raised | waited |
| watched | painted | kissed |
| rubbed | assisted | worked |

**Fill in the blank with the missing word or the word with its ending.**

**1.** buggy + *s* = _____

**2.** _____ +*s* = dollies

**3.** flop + *ed* = _____

**4.** _____ +*ed* = popped

**5.** gray + *s* = _____

**6.** rain + *ed* = _____

Name: _____ Date:_____

# Unit 6 Review: Decodable Story

**Read the following story and then answer the questions.**

Maisy was a vibrant girl who lived on a quiet ranch with her family. They spent their days feeding the pigs, planting seeds, and collecting ripe tomatoes. It was a good life, but Maisy had big dreams away from the ranch.

For many years, Maisy's parents, grandparents, and even great grand-parents had tended the land. It was a big, well-respected ranch, and her family was pleased with the jobs they had. Maisy liked playing with the pigs and seeing the seeds pop up each year, but she had dreams that would take her away from the ranch.

Maisy dreamed of life in a lab. She had seen how viruses affected her pigs, and she wanted to work on finding cures for illnesses that manifested in animals. She had a great brain for facts, and spent her spare time reading about viruses like swine flu.

Maisy had these big dreams, but she was scared to tell her parents that she wanted to leave the ranch. She sat them down and began to explain what she wanted to do. To her shock, her parents smiled and hugged her. They told her how happy they were for her, and they said they would help her begin to apply for programs.

Maisy was so happy, and her parents beamed with happiness for her!

**1.** What did Maisy dream of doing? Why was Maisy afraid to tell her parents?

_____

_____

**2.** What do you dream of doing?

_____

_____

# Unit 6 Post-Test

**Try your best to read the words below.**

| flies | cry | scratched |
|---|---|---|
| go | Alaska | fluent |
| plumped | pennies | dial |
| druid | spilled | family |

**Try your best to read these sentences.**

1. Grab the velvet jacket and denim jeans on your way out.

2. The stuffed animal is made of cotton.

3. You can use the neon paint for your galaxy project.

4. Take a look at the final edits on the menu.

5. Do not get close to the rodents they may have viruses.

**Fill in the blank with the missing word or the word and its ending.**

1. rally + *s* = _____

2. _____ + *s* = copies

3. flop + *ed* = _____

4. _____ + *ed* = tipped

# Unit 7: *R*-Influenced Vowels

## Tips, Tricks, and Things to Know

This unit introduces students to words with *r*-influenced vowels.

### Finger Tapping Syllables

If your students still need the support of finger tapping, here are some examples within an *r*-influenced vowel word. Notice that the *r* is tapped together with the vowel:

| | | |
|---|---|---|
| tiger | 4 taps | t-i(pound) g-er(pound) |
| dollar | 4 taps | d-o-ll(pound) ar(pound) |

### Using Elkonin Boxes with Multisyllabic R-Influenced Vowel Words

Here is how to divide words with *r*-influenced vowels into Elkonin boxes. If students need more practice with breaking down individual sounds, you may choose to break the Elkonin boxes further.

| R-Influenced Vowels in Multisyllabic Words | |
|---|---|
| hard | er |
| doc | tor |

### Dividing Syllables with *R*-Influenced Vowels

Students should continue to use the same syllabication and labeling rules covered in previous units. This unit focuses on a new rule to add to the previously learned material.

*R*-influenced vowels are kept together with the *r*. Encourage your students to label *r*-influenced vowels with the letter *r*.

## Schwa in R-Influenced Vowels

Schwa is a pattern often seen in words with r-influenced vowels. Words like dollar, tiger, and tutor all have the schwa sound. Keep in mind that schwa always occurs in unaccented syllables. For more information about schwa, refer to page 207 in Unit 6.

## Spelling Rules

**-rr Exception:** When there are two r's next to each other in a word, the vowel often keeps its own sound.

**Soft c and g:** If c or g is followed by the vowels e, i, or y, the letter is soft as in the words city and giant.

**-ge and -dge:** Use -dge after a short vowel. Use -ge after a long vowel.

## Guide Words

Guide words are a visual representation that highlight the taught skill. Use these words when referring to a specific skill. By the end of the unit, students will have a total of 21 Concept-Word Connection Cards. Encourage your students to say the pattern followed by the guide word when they review the cards. For example, for the fern card, they would say, "*er*, fern, /er/." Here are the guide words used in this lesson.

1.  *er/ir/ur*: fern, bird, hurt
2.  *ar*: barn, scare, dollar, wart
3.  *or*: corn, world, doctor, core
4.  *ear*: year, pearl, bear
5.  *-rr*: flurry, carry, ferret

Spelling Rule Soft *c* and *g*: city, gem

Spelling Rule *-ge* and *-dge*: huge, fudge

## Sight Words

Here are the sight words covered in this unit: *show, also, around, form, three, small, set, put, end, does, another, well, large, must, big, even, such,* and *because*.

# Unit 7 Pretest

**Read the words below.**

| | | |
|---|---|---|
| barn | world | center |
| number | gently | ledger |
| stirring | scurry | cage |
| gear | pearl | ferret |
| scare | stork | marry |

**Read the following sentences:**

1. He gently carried the caged bird inside his home.

2. You must pay the fare to ride the roller coaster.

3. The slurry mix of sleet and ice will make driving a danger.

4. Tell Jerry to bring his cord for the computer.

5. You may have one swirled ice cream cone after dinner.

**Use the blanks to spell the word illustrated in each bossy *R* picture.**

_____   _____   _____

_____   _____

# Practice Literacy at Home

Dear Parents/Guardians,

Today, we begin Unit 7: *R*-Influenced Vowels. *R*-influenced vowels, also known as bossy *r* vowels, are paired with the letter *r* to create a new sound such as *er*, *ir*, *ur*, *ar*, *or*, and *-ear*. Some of these vowels combined with *r* also make a schwa sound like /er/, such as in the *or* in doctor, the *ar* in dollar, and the *ear* in pearl. When *ar* follows a *w*, it can make the /or/ sound as in war. In *ear*, it can make a long *a* plus *r* sound as in bear. This unit also introduces three different spelling rules, the *-rr* sound, soft *c* and *g*, and words ending in *-ge* and *-dge*. When there are two *r*'s next to each other in a word, the vowel often keeps its own sound as in carry. When learning about soft *c* and *g*, it's important for your child to remember that when *c* or *g* is followed by *e*, *i*, or *y*, the consonant is soft. The end of this unit teaches that *-dge* appears after a short vowel and *-ge* after a long vowel.

If you'd like your child to practice this unit at home, here are the dates for each lesson and some words your child can practice reading, writing, and spelling.

| Dates: | | | | | | | |
|---|---|---|---|---|---|---|---|
| Skills: | er/ir/ur | ar | or | -ear, schwa, /a/ | -rr | soft c/g | -ge/-dge |
| Examples: | fur | war | scorn | fear | blurry | city | cage |
| | paper | dollar | store | pear | carrot | gently | dredge |
| | bird | alarm | doctor | pearl | hurry | center | nudge |
| | stir | warden | world | beard | array | giant | badge |
| | burly | bark | tumor | teardrop | torrid | celery | gage |
| | fern | hare | work | earth | marry | icy | huge |

To make reading and writing even more fun, have your child write a story using some of the words above. Or, encourage them to come up with their own nonsense words using the spelling patterns.

Happy learning!

# Lesson 1 | R-Influenced Vowels *er, ir, & ur*

## *Review and Pretest*

## Introduce the New Concept

This unit introduces students to a new syllable type, *r*-influenced vowels. Also called a bossy *r*, when an *r* is next to a vowel, it "bosses the vowel around" and changes its original sound. Today, we will cover the most common patterns, *er, ir,* and *ur*. These patterns all make the same sound, /er/. While there are no definitive patterns to help students pick which of the three to use, let them know that *er* is the most common form, followed by *ur* and then *ir*, which is not very common at all. Write the following words for your students to see.

| *er* | *ur* | *ir* |
|------|------|------|
| her | slurp | twirl |
| nerve | church | bird |
| clerk | turn | stir |

## Finger Tapping

| swerve | 4 taps | s-w-er-ve |
|--------|--------|-----------|
| first | 4 taps | f-ir-s-t |

## Elkonin Boxes

## Concept-Picture Connection

Guide Word(s): fern, bird, hurt

## Multisensory Connections

| dirt | fir | curb |
|------|-----|------|
| herd | burn | term |

## Sight Words

Create index cards and practice arm tapping for the following words: *show, also, around,* and *form*.

Name: _____  Date: _____

# *R*-Influenced Vowels: *er*, *ir*, & *ur*

**Read each word below.**

| serve | birch | firm |
|-------|-------|------|
| tiger | dinner | slur |
| finger | lurk | verb |
| smirk | kernel | otter |
| verse | lobster | birth |

**Read the sentences and underline the words with the *er/ir/ur* sound.**

1. Turn right when you get to the end of the line.
2. The chirping bird kept the baby awake during her nap!
3. Can you help me make dinner?
4. "I want to go to the surfing contest too," Irma whined.
5. "I do not understand what you mean," I whispered.
6. Irwin and my father had dinner together yesterday.
7. She is third in line to see the tiger.
8. Can you see her twirl her skirt?
9. The toddler will squirt you with the hose if you get too close!
10. "I am so thirsty! Can you get me a glass of water?" pleaded Bertha.

**Fill in the blanks with the correct *er/ir/ur* spelling.**

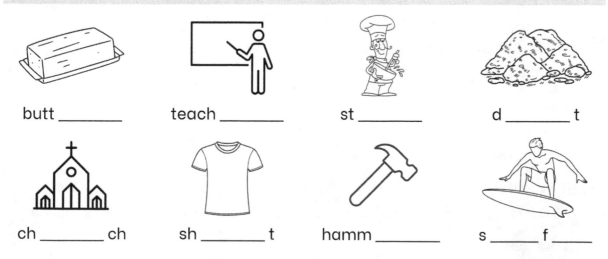

butt _____    teach _____    st _____    d _____ t

ch _____ ch    sh _____ t    hamm _____    s _____ f _____

# Lesson 2 | R-Influenced Vowel *ar*

*Review*

## Introduce the New Concept

Today's lesson focuses on the spelling pattern *ar*. This is different from *er, ir,* and *ur,* which all sound like /er/. *Ar* can make four sounds. Write down the following four words. Encourage students to listen for the different /ar/ sound in each word.

**ar**

| | |
|---|---|
| barn | Barn has the most common /ar/ pattern. This should be the first guess. |
| scare | Scare has a magic *e,* so the *a* has a long *a* sound. There are a few words with the long *a* sound without a magic *e* as in carrot, but they are rare and do not need to be taught explicitly. |
| dollar | Dollar has an *ar* at the end of a multisyllabic word, which makes the *ar* sound like a schwa /er/. |
| wart | In the word wart, the *ar* makes a sound like /or/. This is the least common pattern and occurs when the *ar* follows a *w.* |

## Finger Tapping

| | | |
|---|---|---|
| square | 3 taps | s-qu-are |
| alarm | 4 taps | a(pound) l-ar-m(pound) |

## Elkonin Boxes

| war | den |
|---|---|

## Concept-Picture Connection

Guide Word(s): barn, scare, dollar, wart

## Multisensory Connections

| | | |
|---|---|---|
| dark | swarm | quart |
| charm | sharp | warm |

## Sight Words

Create index cards and practice arm tapping for the following words: *three, small, set,* and *put.*

## Mini Assessment

Ask students to spell the following words: *herd, dark, stir,* and *curl.*

# *R*-Influenced Vowel *ar*

**Read each word below.**

| | | |
|---|---|---|
| stare | war | hare |
| far | hard | chart |
| bark | rare | scar |
| starve | star | alarm |

**Read the sentences and underline the words with the /ar/ sound.**

1. The boy put the pig in the barn.
2. We need to follow the rules when there is a fire alarm.
3. Can you turn on the light? I do not like the dark.
4. How many jars of buttons do you need to finish your quilt?
5. I will try to prepare her, but I do not know how she will fare in the contest.
6. The bugs will swarm that jar of sweets!
7. If you want to win the award, you need to start working on the project now.
8. Carey likes art, and Mara likes math. What is your best subject?
9. There is a sharp glass fragment in your yard. Be careful!
10. The hare was jumping in the yard, but he fled when he saw me.

**Fill in the blank by spelling each *ar* picture.**

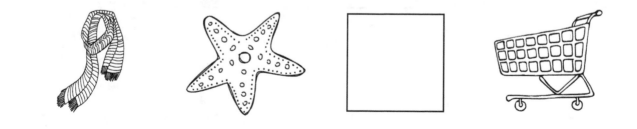

_____   _____   _____   _____

# *R*-Influenced Vowels: *er*, *ir*, *ur*, *ar*
# Mini Assessment

**Read the following words:**

| | | |
|---|---|---|
| stern | hare | alarm |
| award | burn | churn |
| twirl | scare | jar |

**Try your best to spell each word you hear.**

1. _____

2. _____

3. _____

4. _____

## Lesson 3 | R-Influenced Vowel *or*

*Review*

### Introduce the New Concept

The *or* spelling pattern has four primary sound patterns. Write the following words below. Encourage your students to listen for the different sound patterns in the words. Just like *ar*, these words should be taught by commonality.

**or**

| | |
|---|---|
| corn | Corn has the most common /or/ pattern. This should be the first guess. |
| core | Core has a magic *e*, so the *o* has a long *o* sound. |
| doctor | Doctor has an *or* at the end of a multisyllabic word, which makes the *or* sound like a schwa /er/. |
| world | In the word world, the *or* makes a sound like /er/. This is the least common pattern and occurs when the *or* follows a *w*. |

### Finger Tapping

| | | |
|---|---|---|
| rumor | 4 taps | r-u(pound) m-or(pound) |
| thorn | 3 taps | th-or-n |

### Elkonin Boxes

### Concept-Picture Connection

Guide Word(s): corn, world, doctor, core

### Multisensory Connections

| | | |
|---|---|---|
| savor | flavor | tore |
| thorn | cork | worse |

### Sight Words

Create index cards and practice arm tapping for the following words: *end, does, another,* and *well.*

Name: _____ Date: _____

# R-Influenced Vowel *or*

**Read each word below.**

| | | |
|---|---|---|
| humor | fork | contort |
| order | sort | visitor |
| torn | mortal | order |
| horse | port | gator |
| worst | chore | absorb |
| endorse | porch | word |

**Read the sentences and underline the words with the *or* sound.**

1. Can you show me the way to the doctor? My leg pain has gotten worse.

2. This is a formal meal. Please use your fork!

3. Honk the horn when you arrive, and I will run out.

4. The mayor will be at the ribbon cutting for the new visitors' area.

5. The hornets will swarm if you disturb their nest.

6. Is that an ant eating the morsel of corn?

7. I made a mistake on your paper. Please cross out number three on the test.

8. That baby horse was born during the storm last year.

9. The horn and organ are very hard to ignore.

10. The porcupine lives north of the thorn bush.

**Fill in the blank by spelling each *or* picture.**

_____ _____ _____ _____

## Lesson 4 | R-Influenced Vowel *ear*

*Review*

## Introduce the New Concept

This *r*-influenced vowel looks like a vowel team at first glance, but it does not make a typical vowel team sound. This pattern can make three sounds. Write the following words for students to view. Encourage them to listen to the vowel sounds in the following words.

***ear***

| | |
|---|---|
| year | In the word year, we hear a long *e* sound, but it is slightly changed by the *r*. This is the most likely sound option. |
| pearl | In the next word, pearl, there is a schwa sound. This is the second most common sound option. |
| bear | In this pattern, the *ear* makes an /ār/ sound. This is the least common pattern. |

## Finger Tapping

| | | |
|---|---|---|
| beard | 3 taps | b-ear-d |
| early | 3 taps | ear(pound) l-y(pound) |

## Elkonin Boxes

| re | hearse |
|---|---|

## Concept-Picture Connection

Guide Word(s): pearl, bear, year

## Multisensory Connections

| | | |
|---|---|---|
| near | heard | yearn |
| tear (long a) | sear | swear |

## Sight Words

Create index cards and practice arm tapping for the following words: *even, such, because, large, must,* and *big*.

## Mini Assessment

Ask students to spell the following words: *smear, horn, doctor,* and *learn*.

# R-Influenced Vowel *ear*

**Read each word below.**

| | | |
|---|---|---|
| ear | earth | pearly |
| hear | gear | swear |
| dreary | earl | teardrop |
| smear | fear | earn |

**Read the sentences and underline the words with the *or* sound.**

1. Please stay on the trail. There have been wild animals, such as bears and alligators, in the area.

2. Do not worry! I will stay near you the whole time.

3. We need to put the shears back after we trim the tree.

4. The meeting is set for early Monday morning because I have to go to the doctor.

5. Those three girls are learning about the earthworms.

6. Can you hear me in the back? I am going to start speaking about the Earl of Essex.

7. The pear is good, even with peanut butter on it!

8. She is going to wear the costume inspired by the Earth.

9. Wipe away your tears. It will all be okay!

10. There is a smear of ink on the gear. We will need to wash it.

**Read the sentences and fill in the blank with the correct *ear* word from the word bank.**

1. What do you want for your birthday this _____?

2. Did the dog _____ up your socks?

3. You may need to shave your _____.

4. Wear the _____ with the dress.

5. Clean the glass so you can see the yard _____.

| |
|---|
| tear |
| earrings |
| beard |
| year |
| clearly |

Name: _____  Date: _____

# *R*-Influenced Vowels: *or*, *ear*
# Mini Assessment

**Read the following words:**

| | | |
|---|---|---|
| clear | fear | porch |
| earn | mortal | bore |
| port | earl | pearl |
| worse | dreary | gator |

**Try your best to spell each word you hear.**

1. _____

2. _____

3. _____

4. _____

## Spelling Rule | -*rr* Exception

*Review*

### Introduce the New Concept

Instruct students to copy down the following new spelling rule in their Orton-Gillingham notebooks.

**-*rr* Exception:** When a word contains two *r*'s next to each other, the vowel often keeps its own sound.

*Exception:* The pattern -*err* sounds like /ār/ as in the words errand and terry.

For example, in the word car, we hear a clear /ar/ pattern. However, when that word is changed to carry, we hear the long *a* sound again. Keep in mind that there are some words with the -*rr* pattern that still have an expected *r*-influenced vowel sound. Students may have an easier time remembering this rule if you explain that together, the -*rr* are best friends. When they are together, they are busy playing and they have less time to boss the vowels around!

### Elkonin Boxes

| mar | ry |
|-----|----|

### Concept-Picture Connection

Guide Word(s): flurry, carry, and ferret

### Multisensory Connections

| | |
|-----|-----|
| blurry | embarrass |
| arrest | hurry |
| barrel | scurry |

## Spelling Rule | Soft *c & g*

*Review*

### Introduce the New Concept

Instruct students to copy down the following new spelling rule in their Orton-Gillingham notebooks.

**Soft *c & g*:** If *c* or *g* is followed by the vowels *e*, *i*, or *y*, the letter is soft.

*Exceptions*: Words such as gear, get, girl, tiger, and gift.

Review the words below:

| soft *c* | soft *g* |
|----------|----------|
| city | gem |
| center | gist |
| cycle | gyrate |

### Elkonin Boxes

| cir | cus |
|-----|-----|

### Concept-Picture Connection

Guide Word(s): city, gem

### Multisensory Connections

| | |
|--------|--------|
| advance | pace |
| giant | circus |
| gulch | gum |

## Spelling Rule | -*ge* versus -*dge*

*Review*

### Introduce the New Concept

Prior to teaching this new spelling rule, it may be helpful to review the *k/-ck* and the *ch/-tch* rules since they follow similar guidelines.

Instruct students to copy down the following spelling rule in their Orton-Gillingham notebooks:

**-*dge*/-*ge*:** Use -*dge* after a short vowel. Use -*ge* after a long vowel or consonant.

Review the words below:

| -*dge* | -*ge* |
|--------|-------|
| fudge | huge |
| hedge | strange |
| wedge | wage |

### Elkonin Boxes

| re | venge |
|----|-------|

### Concept-Picture Connection

Guide Word(s): huge, fudge

### Multisensory Connections

| | |
|---|---|
| bridge | lodge |
| cage | badge |
| surge | rage |

# -rr, Soft c & g, -ge versus -dge

Read each word below.

### - rr Words

| | | |
|---|---|---|
| array | marry | scurry |
| carrot | Larry | current |
| hurray | narrate | quarry |
| churro | horrid | Harry |

### Soft c/g Words

| | | |
|---|---|---|
| gym | rice | center |
| cent | game | cold |
| gypsy | recent | gulp |
| huge | gallop | cash |

### -ge/ -dge Words

| | | |
|---|---|---|
| plunge | change | lunge |
| huge | edge | indulge |
| hinge | sledge | rage |

Spell the word illustrated in each picture below.

_____    _____    _____

_____    _____

# Unit 7 Review: Decodable Story

**Read the following story and then answer the questions below.**

Nora was an angry pig. Her home had just been huffed and puffed down by a hungry wolf. She and her brothers were okay, and they managed to scare away the wolf, but now she had to put together a new home.

She had no idea that a home constructed of sticks would be a bad idea since she had never seen a wolf in the city she lived in, and certainly not a wolf with lungs that could puff down a home! Nora and her brothers, Larry and Hugo, decided that they would make a larger home that they could all live in together just in case the wolf came back.

They gathered cement, bricks, and rebar to create the strongest home they could think up. They set to work laying bricks, dumping cement, and reinforcing with metal rebar. They each looked for ways that a wolf could enter, and made those areas stronger. Their jobs let them take time off to get back on their feet. After many weeks of work, their home was done.

As Nora looked up at their new home, she was no longer mad. In fact, she was grateful. While Nora had lost her first home because of the wolf, she and her brothers were not hurt. They escaped safely. They had the time and funds to build a new home. Their jobs let them take the time they needed to set up their home.

This thinking led Nora and her brothers to open a charity to help other displaced animals. They would help animals in need make new homes after disasters happened to them. Nora was able to turn her bad luck into something that would help those around her, and for that, she was truly thankful.

**1.** Who ruined Nora's home? How?

_____

_____

**2.** How did Nora and her brothers turn their misfortune into good?

_____

_____

Name: _____     Date: _____

# Unit 7 Post-Test

**Read the following words:**

| | | |
|---|---|---|
| warn | pork | cent |
| stranger | gelatin | badger |
| swirling | flurry | stage |
| dear | pearl | terry |
| pare | port | carry |

**Read the following sentences:**

1. Feed the ferret in his cage or he will make a huge mess.

2. You can enter the scary home, but I am too fearful.

3. Play with the furry puppies later. Now you must do your homework.

4. We learned that a century is a hundred years.

5. Stir the mix, then dredge the chicken with it.

**On the blanks below, spell the r-influenced word illustrated in the picture.**

_____    _____    _____

_____    _____

# Unit 8: Diphthongs and Advanced Vowel Patterns

## Tips, Tricks, and Things to Know

This unit introduces students to words with diphthongs and advanced vowel patterns.

### Finger Tapping Syllables

If your students still require the support of finger tapping, here are some examples found within words that contain an advanced vowel. Notice that the diphthongs and vowel teams are tapped together:

| | | |
|---|---|---|
| author | 3 taps | au(pound) th-or(pound) |
| spoiling | 5 taps | s-p-oi-l(pound) ing(pound) |

### Using Elkonin Boxes with Diphthongs and Advanced Vowel Patterns

Here is how to divide words with advanced vowels and diphthongs into Elkonin boxes. If students need more practice with breaking down individual sounds, you may choose to break the Elkonin boxes further.

| Advanced Vowels/Diphthongs in Multisyllabic Words | |
|---|---|
| Au | gust |
| don | key |

### Dividing Syllables with Diphthongs and Advanced Vowel Patterns

As a reminder, students should use the same syllabication and labeling rules covered in previous units. You may want to suggest they review the Tips, Tricks, and Things to Know sections in Units 3–7.

Advanced vowel teams and diphthongs are kept together. Diphthongs maintain their sound regardless of their position in a word.

## Spelling Rules

**ie/ei:** *I* before *e* except after *c* or in words that sound like *-ay*.

*Exceptions*: Words such as caffeine, species, height, and ancient.

## Spelling Generalizations

In general, if a diphthong ends in a consonant such as *aw, oy, ow, ew,* or *ey*, it most likely appears at the middle or end of a word.

## Guide Words

Guide words are a visual representation that highlight the taught skill. Use these words when referring to a specific skill. By the end of the unit, students will have a total of 18 Concept-Word Connection Cards. When they review the cards, they should say the pattern followed by the guide word. For example, for the pool card, they would say, "oo, pool, /oo/." These are the guide words used in the lesson:

1. *au/aw*: draw, astronaut
2. *oi/oy*: boy, coil
3. *ou/ow*: owl, snow, ouch
4. *oo*: pool, book
5. *ea*: break, head
6. *eu/ew*: feud, chew
7. *igh, eigh, ey*: night, monkey, sleigh

Spelling Rule *ie/ei*: cookie, receive

## Sight Words

At this point in the book, most sight words are now phonetic. If your students struggle with any sight words, teach them explicitly. Refer to the How to Use This Book section on page 15 for ideas. If not, choose words that your student is struggling with based on their writing samples. Refer to the Unit 8 sight words on page 291.

# Unit 8 Pretest

**Read the words below.**

| | | |
|---|---|---|
| faucet | crook | feud |
| sauce | room | sleigh |
| boil | heal | slight |
| coy | wear | key |
| count | threat | piece |
| crowd | pew | lei |

**Read the following sentences:**

1. Remember not to chew too loudly at the event tonight.

2. She showed us how to paint flowers last August.

3. Do you think it will start to snow at dawn? I heard we are supposed to get eight inches!

4. The red sauce almost destroyed the laundry.

5. Did you see the reindeer near the valley?

**Spell each word illustrated in the picture.**

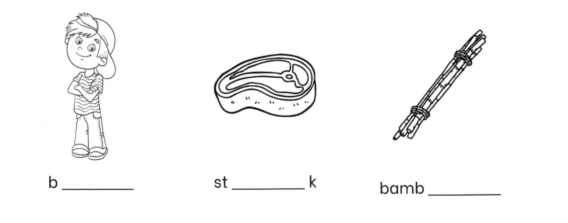

b _____        st _____ k        bamb _____

# Practice Literacy at Home

Dear Parents/Guardians,

We have started our journey into Unit 8: Diphthongs and Advanced Vowel Patterns. Diphthongs are two vowels put together in which one sound glides into another. The diphthongs your child will be learning are *au/aw* (as in August, claw), *oi/oy* (boil, boy), *ou/ow* (ouch, how, snow), *oo* (pool, hook), *ea* (health, break), and *eu/ew* (feud, dew). The last lesson focuses on the sounds of *igh*, *eigh*, and *ey* as in night, sleigh, and key. The unit ends with an *ie/ei* spelling rule.

If you'd like your child to practice this unit at home, here are the dates for each lesson as well as some words your child can practice reading, writing, and spelling.

| Dates: | | | | | | | | |
|---|---|---|---|---|---|---|---|---|
| Skills: | *au/aw* | *oi/oy* | *ou/ow* | *oo* | *ea* | *eu/ew* | *igh/eigh/ ey* | *ie/ei* |
| Examples: | faucet | toys | crow | pool | health | sleuth | night | piece |
| | August | destroy | couch | brook | steak | chew | slight | ceiling |
| | fault | boiler | found | stool | treat | grew | weigh | thief |
| | claw | roil | prowl | football | break | feud | hockey | achieve |
| | straw | boy | stow | crook | sneak | stew | kidney | vein |
| | drawn | coil | sound | roofer | deaf | few | freight | rein |

To make reading and writing even more fun, have your child write a story using some of the words above. Or, encourage your child to come up with their own nonsense words using the spelling patterns.

Happy learning!

## Lesson 1 | Diphthongs *au* & *aw*

### *Review and Pretest*

### Introduce the New Concept

Students have now covered all of the regular vowel teams. Today's unit introduces diphthongs. Diphthongs are vowel sounds that contain two letters, with at least one vowel. They do not make an expected vowel sound. Instead, they have two sounds that "glide into each other.

Encourage students to listen to the vowel sounds in the following words:

| *au* | *aw* |
|------|------|
| August | straw |
| cause | law |
| vault | spawn |

For many diphthongs there are generalizations students can refer to in order to determine which pattern to use in spelling. One general rule is that if a diphthong ends in a consonant such as *aw*, *oy*, *ow*, *ew*, or *ey*, it is most likely to appear at the middle or end of a word.

The pattern *au* is always seen at the beginning or middle of a word. *Aw* is most often found at the end of a word.

### Finger Tapping

| straw | 4 taps | s-t-r-aw |
|-------|--------|----------|
| author | 3 taps | au(pound) th-or(pound) |

### Elkonin Boxes

| pau | per |
|-----|-----|

### Concept-Picture Connection

Guide Word(s): draw, astronaut

### Multisensory Connections

| fault | vault |
|-------|-------|
| saw | crawl |
| thaw | haul |

# Diphthongs *au* & *aw*

**Read each word below.**

| | | |
|---|---|---|
| hawk | seesaw | brawl |
| sprawl | nautical | saucer |
| slaw | fauna | jaw |
| crawfish | prawn | flaw |

**Read the sentences and circle the *au/aw* words.**

1. August is the hottest month of the year in many states.

2. "Please tell me what the sauce has in it," Audie asked.

3. The old washing room faucet needs to be replaced so we can do the laundry.

4. That crawfish looks the same as the one we saw last Monday at dawn. It has big claws!

5. The scrawny hawk needs to hunt for his meal before he gets too weak.

6. My aunt makes the best coleslaw!" Auden exclaimed.

7. Paul and Shawn are going to see the author speak at the coffee shop.

8. August asked, "Are there any prawns left for my dinner?"

9. I applaud your efforts in learning to read!

10. The pup snacked on his rawhide while his mother yawned.

**Spell the *au/aw* word illustrated in each picture.**

   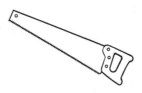

_____  _____  _____  _____

# Lesson 2 | Diphthongs *oi* & *oy*

*Review*

## Introduce the New Concept

Encourage students to listen to the vowel sounds in the following words:

| *oi* | *oy* |
|------|------|
| boil | joy |
| toil | ploy |
| join | coy |

The pattern *oi* is always seen at the beginning or middle of a word. *Oy* is most often found at the end of a word.

## Finger Tapping

| | | |
|---|---|---|
| broil | 4 taps | b-r-oi-l |
| employ | 5 taps | e-m(pound) p-l-oy(pound) |

## Elkonin Boxes

| toi | let |
|-----|-----|

## Concept-Picture Connection

Guide Word(s): boy, coil

## Multisensory Connections

| | | |
|---|---|---|
| hoist | spoil | rejoin |
| joy | boy | noise |

## Mini Assessment

Ask students to spell the following words: *foil*, *straw*, *soy*, and *auger*.

# Diphthongs *oi* & *oy*

**Read each word below.**

| | | |
|---|---|---|
| turmoil | destroy | royal |
| coy | soil | soy |
| hoist | coil | toy |
| ahoy | noisy | appoint |

**Read the sentences and circle the *oi/oy* words.**

1. The boy is playing in the garden soil.

2. Do not leave the milk out or it will spoil.

3. The royal queen rushed through the noisy city.

4. "I think I hear a voice," Moira whispered. "No, that is just the pigs oinking," the boy replied.

5. I want pasta for dinner, so I need to boil some water.

6. "Please follow me so you can join the other children," the teacher instructed.

7. "She went to the store yesterday to pick out a new toy," Sam said.

8. Can you put the silver coins in the piggy bank?

9. I know you will enjoy your time at the cabin. I think you made a good choice!

10. I think we should avoid that spot. It is too noisy!

**Spell the *oi/oy* word illustrated in the picture.**

_____     _____     _____     _____

Name: _____ Date: _____

# Diphthongs *au/aw* & *oi/oy*
# Mini Assessment

**Read the following words:**

| | | |
|---|---|---|
| slaw | August | prawn |
| moist | claw | destroy |
| ploy | point | saucer |

**Try your best to spell each word you hear.**

1. _____

2. _____

3. _____

4. _____

# Lesson 3 | Diphthongs *ou* & *ow*

*Review*

## Introduce the New Concept

The patterns *ou* and *ow* have several sounds. This lesson reviews the three most common sounds. Encourage students to listen to the vowel sounds in the following words:

| *ou* | *ow* | *ow* (ō) |
|------|------|----------|
| ouch | how | snow |
| stout | crowd | elbow |
| found | prowl | show |

The pattern *ou* is always at the beginning or middle of a word. *Ow* is most often found at the end of a word or before the letters *l*, *n*, or *d*.

After reviewing the most common sounds, review the other sound options for *ou* below. These will not be taught in an additional lesson since they are relatively uncommon in comparison to the more traditional *ou*/*ow* sounds.

*Ou* can also make a long /o/ sound as in four, an /oo/ sound as in routine, and a short /u/ sound as in tough, but it most often makes the /ow/ sound.

You may want to add the following words to your list to demonstrate the other fairly rare sounds of *ou*:

| mourn, court | you, group | cousin, country |
|--------------|------------|-----------------|

## Finger Tapping

| | | |
|---|---|---|
| brown | 4 taps | b-r-ow-n |
| founder | 5 taps | f-ou-n-d(pound) er(pound) |

## Elkonin Boxes

| re | count |
|----|-------|

## Concept-Picture Connection

Guide Word(s): owl, snow, ouch

## Multisensory Connections

| | | |
|---|---|---|
| below | house | shout |
| scowl | gown | cow |

# Diphthongs *ou & ow*

**Read each word below.**

| | | |
|---|---|---|
| glow | announce | how |
| flour | out | down |
| account | frown | yellow |
| towel | throw | gown |
| blow | pillow | couch |

**Read the sentences and underline the *ou/ow* words.**

1. When you finish cleaning the cow pen, please take a shower.

2. I found an owl on that tree below the branch!

3. The clown made a funny joke about that yellow crown.

4. The round toy is rolling down the driveway.

5. Please tell me about the house you are staying in.

6. "OUCH!" the girl yelled as she fell off the swing.

7. There is no need to frown, we will decide how to fix the snow problem!

8. Can you count the cups of flour as I dump them in the mixer?

9. The mouse needs to hide from the owl unless it wants to be dinner!

10. We need to round up the hounds before the storm comes.

**Circle the correct spelling of each picture.**

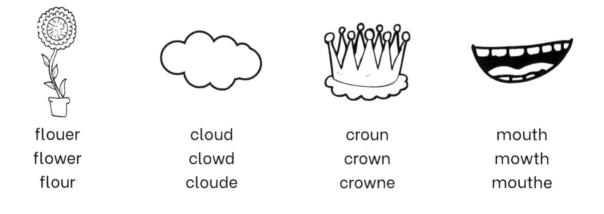

| | | | |
|---|---|---|---|
| flouer | cloud | croun | mouth |
| flower | clowd | crown | mowth |
| flour | cloude | crowne | mouthe |

# Lesson 4 | Diphthong *oo*

## *Review*

### Introduce the New Concept

Encourage students to listen to the vowel sounds in the following words:

| *oo* (long) | *oo* (short) |
|:---:|:---:|
| pool | good |
| roof | brook |
| noon | look |

The pattern *oo* is unlike some of the other diphthongs because it sounds like a long *u* as in dune or rule, in its most common form, long *oo*. It is also very similar to a short *u* in its second most common form (as in book). The pattern long *oo* should be a second guess after attempting a *uCe* pattern.

Both of these patterns are most likely to occur in the middle of a word. If you hear this sound at the end of a word, it is likely spelled with a *u* silent *e*, or a *ue*.

### Finger Tapping

| | | |
|:---:|:---:|:---:|
| scoop | 4 taps | s-c-oo-p |
| football | 5 taps | f-oo-t(pound) b-all(pound) |

### Elkonin Boxes

| good | bye |
|:---:|:---:|

### Concept-Picture Connection

Guide Word(s): pool, book

### Multisensory Connections

| | | |
|:---:|:---:|:---:|
| good | foot | scoop |
| rooster | roof | scooter |

### Mini Assessment

Ask students to spell the following words: *rooster*, *pouch*, *snow*, and *book*.

# Diphthong *oo*

Name: _____    Date: _____

**Read each word below.**

| | | |
|---|---|---|
| smooth | cook | food |
| too | fool | shoot |
| cookout | shook | stood |
| loose | hook | root |

**Read the sentences and underline the *oo* words.**

1. The woodpecker shook the soot off as it darted out of the flue.

2. Let's take a dip in the pool around three o'clock this afternoon!

3. "Can I bring food to class on my birthday?" the third grader asked.

4. Please put the broom on the hook in the closet.

5. "There is nothing better than reading a good book at the pool!" her mom exclaimed.

6. "Can you set the counter? The spoons are in the small cupboard to the left," Mona said to Will.

7. The moon lit up the water in the brook.

8. Would you like to have a cookout this afternoon?

9. The dog began to woof as he saw the crook approaching the home.

10. That rooster crows all day long.

**Spell the word for each picture. Circle all of the pictures that have an *oo* diphthong.**

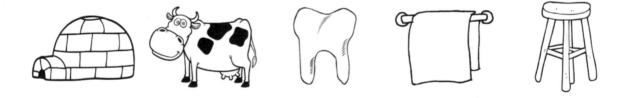

_____   _____   _____   _____   _____

# Diphthongs *ou/ow* & *oo*
# Mini Assessment

**Read the following words:**

| | |
|---|---|
| throw | broom |
| spoon | nook |
| pillow | cookout |
| how | zoom |
| couch | voucher |

**Try your best to spell each word you hear.**

1. _____

2. _____

3. _____

4. _____

# Lesson 5 | Diphthong *ea*

*Review*

## Introduce the New Concept

Encourage students to listen to the vowel sounds in the following words:

| *ea* (long *e*) | *ea* (short *e*) | *ea* (long *a*) |
|---|---|---|
| beach | health | steak |
| treat | bread | break |
| bean | deaf | great |

Students already learned *ea*'s most common sound, long *e*, as represented by the index card beach, which they made in Unit 5. The next most common sound that *ea* makes is a short *e*. The last sound *ea* makes is long *a*. This is not a common variation, so it should be a student's last guess when they hear a long *a* within a word.

All of these patterns are most commonly found in the middle of words.

## Finger Tapping

| | | |
|---|---|---|
| stealth | 5 taps | s-t-ea-l-th |
| great | 4 taps | g-r-ea-t |

## Elkonin Boxes

| break | fast |
|---|---|

## Concept-Picture Connection

Guide Word(s): break, head, beach (beach was covered in Unit 5)

## Multisensory Connections

| | | |
|---|---|---|
| clean | wear | meant |
| spread | death | cream |

# Diphthong *ea*

**Read each word below.**

| | | |
|---|---|---|
| threat | wear | breath |
| teach | meant | neat |
| meat | cheat | seal |
| stealth | steak | scream |

**Read the sentences and circle the *ea* words.**

1. May I have another sweet treat for breakfast?" Leana asked.

2. "What does she have on her calendar this week? I would like to plan a day at the beach," Jean inquired.

3. Can you teach me how to speak Spanish?

4. Will you have time to read to the end of that book before class starts?

5. The farmers picked the peaches off the trees just in time for the city fair.

6. "That bakery has the best bread in town!" he exclaimed.

7. Some people like to have their steak cooked well-done.

8. Tread carefully over that ice. It may be weak since the weather is heating up.

9. My grandma loves to visit the flea market on Sea Avenue.

10. Try to catch your breath during our break, because it will be a while before we can stop again.

**Write the word in the correct column.**

| long *e* (beach) | short *e* (health) | long *a* (steak) |
|---|---|---|
| | | |

leaf          bread          bear          team          weapon

great                  steal                  dread

# Lesson 6 | Diphthongs *eu* & *ew*

## Review

### Introduce the New Concept

This lesson reviews the *ui* and *ue* pattern in addition to teaching two new spelling rules for the *eu/ew* pattern. If students need a refresher, review the *ui* and *ue* lesson on page 188 in Unit 5. Encourage students to listen to the vowel sounds in the following words:

**Review**

| *ui* | *ue* |
|------|------|
| fruit | blue |
| suit | rescue |

**Introduce**

| *eu* | *ew* |
|------|------|
| feud | chew |
| sleuth | new |

The patterns *ui* and *eu* are always seen at the beginning or middle of a word. The patterns *ew* and *ue* are most commonly found at the end of words. The pattern *eu* is not very common. It is most often seen within scientific concepts such as in neuron and neurology.

### Finger Tapping

| neutral | 5 taps | n-eu(pound) t-r-al(pound) |
|---------|--------|---------------------------|
| flew | 3 taps | f-l-ew |

### Elkonin Boxes

| jew | el |
|-----|----|

### Concept-Picture Connection

Guide Word(s): feud, chew, rescue, clue, fruit

### Multisensory Connections

| recruit | feudal | rescue |
|---------|--------|--------|
| stew | threw | grew |

### Mini Assessment

Ask students to spell the following words: *sleuth*, *few*, *great*, and *threat*.

# Diphthongs *eu* & *ew*

## Read each word below.

| | | |
|---|---|---|
| sleuth | blew | brew |
| statue | blue | suitcase |
| dew | feud | new |
| juice | crew | due |

## Read the sentences and underline the *eu*/*ew* words.

1. Andrew will wait for the bus by the large statue.

2. We must remember to pack the big case of juice for the game.

3. Are you due for a doctor's visit? I can make it for Tuesday if you would like.

4. The hairstylist worked to make sure that Sue's new haircut was even at the ends.

5. John will brew the coffee while Sue packs the suitcase.

6. "When I give you the cue, walk out onto the stage and begin reciting your lines," the theater teacher stated.

7. While Drew tried to recruit the student on to his rugby team, Nelly suggested that he would be better suited to soccer.

8. The teacher hurriedly explained that the paper was due after the break, as her students filed out of the classroom.

## Circle the correct spelling of each picture.

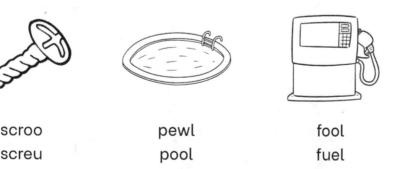

| | | | |
|---|---|---|---|
| scroo | pewl | fool | stew |
| screu | pool | fuel | steu |
| screw | peul | feul | stoo |

# Diphthongs *ea*, *eu*, & *ew*
# Mini Assessment

**Read the following words:**

| | | |
|---|---|---|
| head | stealth | chew |
| blue | bear | steak |
| lean | fruit | dew |
| hue | feud | neutral |

**Try your best to spell each word you hear.**

1. _____

2. _____

3. _____

4. _____

## Lesson 7 | Diphthongs *igh, eigh, & ey*

*Review*

## Introduce the New Concept

Encourage students to listen to the vowel sounds in the following words:

| *igh* | *eigh* | *ey* |
|---|---|---|
| night | sleigh | monkey |
| high | neighbor | kidney |
| flight | weight | galley |

The patterns *igh* and *eigh* are always seen at the middle or end of a word. *Ey* is only found at the end of a word. None of these patterns are very common.

## Finger Tapping

| parsley | 5 taps | p-ar(pound) s-l-ey(pound) |
|---|---|---|
| insight | 5 taps | i-n(pound) s-igh-t(pound) |

## Elkonin Boxes

| neigh | bor |
|---|---|

## Concept-Picture Connection

Guide Word(s): night, monkey, sleigh

## Multisensory Connections

| beige | tonight | highness |
|---|---|---|
| chimney | donkey | weight |

# Diphthongs *igh*, *eigh*, & *ey*

**Read each word below.**

| | | |
|---|---|---|
| daylight | sigh | frighten |
| bright | Mickey | volley |
| weigh | freight | chimney |
| key | sight | eight |

**Read the sentences and underline the *igh*, *eigh*, and *ey* words.**

1. Ann and Mickey play volleyball at eight p.m. every Tuesday night at the park.

2. Here is some chutney for your grilled fish.

3. That man will turn on the tightrope. He is so high above the ground!

4. Our parsley has grown well this year because of all the rain.

5. The lightning looks amazing in the night sky.

6. "Kelsey, please pick up your hockey gear," her mother said with a weighted sigh.

7. Our volleyball team has a hard fight against the other team, but I think we can win!

8. If we hurry, we might have time to catch the night train to the city.

9. Sadly, a burglar came and took her bike between midnight and seven in the morning. We will remain on the lookout for him!

**Fill in the blanks with the correct *igh*, *eigh*, or *ey* spelling.**

sl _____

turk _____

f _____ t

## Spelling Rule | *ie & ei*

*Review*

## Introduce the New Concept

Prior to teaching this new spelling rule, it may be helpful to review the other sounds of long *e* (*ea*, *ee*, *ey*, *y*, and *e-e*). This may help students better understand this new rule.

Instruct students to copy down the following spelling rule in their Orton-Gillingham notebooks.

***ei/ie***: *i* before *e* except after *c* or in words that sound like *-ay*.

*Exceptions*: Words such as caffeine, species, height, ancient, friend, and leisure.

Review the words below:

| **ie** | **ei** |
|:---:|:---:|
| hygiene | ceiling |
| grief | eight |

## Elkonin Boxes

| con | ceit |
|---|---|

## Concept-Picture Connection

Guide Word(s): cookie, sleigh (from previous lesson), receive

## Multisensory Connections

|  |  |  |
|:---:|:---:|:---:|
| feint | thief | pierce |
| deceive | moxie | vein |

# Spelling *ie* versus *ei*

**Read each word below.**

| | | |
|---|---|---|
| neighbor | priest | niece |
| chief | weight | relieved |
| receive | deceit | ceiling |
| achieve | sleigh | conceited |

**Using the pictures as clues, fill in the blank with either *ie* or *ei* to spell each word correctly.**

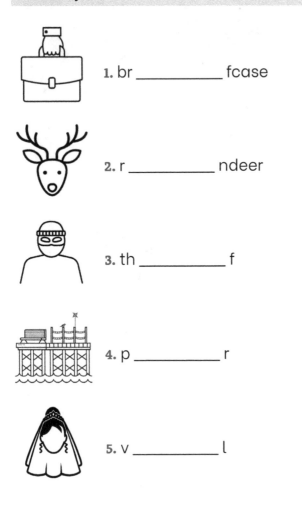

1. br _____ fcase

2. r _____ ndeer

3. th _____ f

4. p _____ r

5. v _____ l

Name: _____  Date: _____

# Unit 8 Review: Decodable Story

**Read the following story and then answer the questions below.**

It was a hot August day, and Loxie and Junie were headed to the pool for the town's big event, "Flick and Float." The girls had their swimsuits, rafts, and pool noodles ready to go. The town was playing a scary film about sharks, and it would start just as it got dark.

Their siblings, Florence and Gideon, had plans of their own. They were also planning to head to the pool, but not watch the film. Rather than watching the sharks on the screen, they planned to "be the sharks." They had been preparing for this night for several weeks. They crafted realistic looking fins using foam and spray paint. Both of their sisters were terrified of sharks, and this was the perfect chance to scare them.

Loxie and Junie hopped into the pool and swam toward the screen just as the flick came on. A shark zoomed across the screen, and Gideon and Florence took the opportunity to crawl into the pool wearing their fins and gray swimsuits. They dove down under their sisters' rafts and gave them a little tap. Loxie turned to Junie and whispered, "Did you feel that?" Junie turned pale. A shark leaped up on the movie and someone screamed "FINS!" behind them. Just then, something grabbed Junie's foot. "OUCH!" she bellowed.

Loxie zoomed to the side of the pool, convinced that a shark was in the pool. Junie and the rest of the attendants at "Flick and Float," followed her at a rapid pace until they saw two little heads pop up out of the water. It was Florence and Gideon! They had planned a prank just to scare their sisters, but it had scared the whole pool instead.

After everyone at the pool had a chance to catch their breath, and share a few stern words with the shark impersonators, they got back in the pool to continue the film. While Florence and Gideon would not play another prank like that again, it was pretty funny to see the looks on their sisters' faces!

**1.** What did Florence and Gideon do? What happened?

_____

_____

**2.** What would you do if you were Loxie and Junie?

_____

_____

# Unit 8 Post-Test

Name: _____   Date: _____

**Try your best to read the words below.**

| | | |
|---|---|---|
| taut | shook | feud |
| sauce | broom | eighty |
| toil | steal | frighten |
| soy | break | valley |
| mount | sweat | piece |
| cower | drew | rein |

**Try your best to read these sentences.**

1. The ship's crew yelled to the passengers to board the boat so they could complete a safety demo.

2. The morning dew coated the grass with a glittery shine that looked pretty in the sun's rays.

3. The bear looked like he weighed over a thousand pounds!

4. The hockey game is tonight at eight.

5. Believe me, you can put soy sauce on steak.

**Spell each word illustrated in the picture below.**

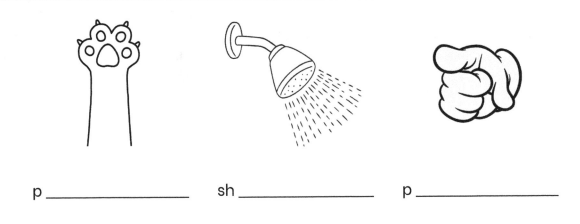

p _____    sh _____    p _____

# Unit 9: Consonant -*le* and Alternate Spellings

## Tips, Tricks, and Things to Know

The final unit introduces students to words with the last syllable pattern, consonant -*le*. They will also learn about alternate spellings including common suffixes, silent letters, and other unusual patterns.

### Finger Tapping Syllables

If your students still require the support of finger tapping, here are a couple of examples found within some of the concepts taught in this unit:

| | | |
|---|---|---|
| vacation | 5 taps | v-a(pound) c-a(pound) tion(pound) |
| measure | 3 taps | m-ea(pound) sure(pound) |

### Using Elkonin Boxes with Consonant -*le* and Alternate Spelling Words

Here is how to divide words with consonant -*le* into Elkonin boxes. Notice that the last three letters of any word with -*le* are their own syllable, except in the case of -*stle*. If students need more practice with breaking down individual sounds, you may choose to break the Elkonin boxes further.

**Consonant -*le***

| | |
|---|---|
| hud | dle |
| sta | ble |
| whi | stle |

**Alternate Spellings**

| | |
|---|---|
| in | jure |
| rhi | no |

## Dividing Syllables with Consonant -*le* and Alternate Spellings

Students should use the same syllabication and labeling rules covered in previous units. For more information refer your students to the Tips, Tricks, and Things to Know sections in Units 3–8.

Consonant -*le* is always divided as its own syllable. The only exceptions are in words like whistle or trickle, which each have two consonants followed by -*le*. These patterns still "close in" the vowel, causing it to make a short sound.

puddle
v  c -cle

cable
v  -cle

tumble
v  c -cle

### Spelling Rules

There are no spelling rules taught in this unit. Take this time to review previously introduced spelling rules.

### Guide Words

Guide words are a visual representation that highlight the taught skill. Use these words when referring to a specific skill. By the end of the unit, students will have a total of 21 Concept-Word Connection Cards. When they review the cards, they should say the pattern followed by the guide word. For example, for the *ph* card, they would say, "*ph*, phone, /f/." These are the guide words used in the lesson:

1. Consonant Plus -*le*: castle, stable, puddle
2. -*ure*, -*sure*, -*ture*: measure, nature, injure
3. -*que* /k/, hard *ch* /k/, soft *ch* /sh/, & *ph*: antique, school, chef, phone
4. *ti*, *si*, *ci*: vacation, profession, delicious, television
5. Silent letter pairs: rhino, ghost, lamb, autumn, knight, gnome, wren

### Sight Words

At this point in the book, most sight words are now phonetic. If your students struggle with any of the words in the Unit 9 list, teach them explicitly. If not, choose words that your students are struggling with based on their writing samples. Refer to the Unit 9 sight words on page 291.

# Unit 9 Pretest

**Read the words below.**

| | | |
|---|---|---|
| circle | unique | numb |
| waddle | sphere | ghoul |
| moisture | foundation | knife |
| conjure | permission | gnat |
| fissure | fusion | wrist |
| chef | delicious | |
| ache | rhombus | |

**Try your best to read these sentences.**

1. The first-grade class spent the week learning about the frog life cycle.

2. First, we need to measure the smaller castle, before we can construct a larger one.

3. Send the laundry down the chute and it will get done by tonight.

4. Can we buy the same professional knives the butcher uses? They would make cooking a lot easier!

5. Write a paragraph about your vacation to the Irish castle.

**Read the words below. For the silent pairs, underline the silent letter and circle the letter that makes the sound.**

rhyme            reign            wrinkle

ghost            crumbs

# Practice Literacy at Home

Dear Parents/Guardians,

We've made it to our last unit, Unit 9: Consonant *-le* and Alternate Spellings! This unit introduces difficult sounds and spelling patterns. The unit begins with a review of how to read words with a consonant plus *-le* ending, such as in the word table. Next, we review how to read sounds such as *-ure*, *-sure*, and *-ture* as in creature, conjure, and fissure. Then your child will learn the /k/ sound of *-que* as in antique, the hard /k/ and soft sounds of *ch* and /sh/ as in character and chef, and the sound of *ph* as in phone. The next lesson reviews the sounds of *ti*, *si*, and *ci*, as in the words vacation, division, and delicious. The final lesson focuses on the most common silent letter pairs: *gh*, *gn*, *kn*, *mb*, *mn*, *rh*, and *wr*. By the end of this unit, your child should be able to read most words with accuracy!

If you'd like your child to practice this unit at home, here are the dates for each lesson and some words your child can practice reading, writing, and spelling.

| Dates: | | | | | |
|---|---|---|---|---|---|
| Skills: | consonant plus -le | -ure/ -sure/ -ture | -que, ch, ph | ti, si, ci | common silent letter pairs |
| Examples: | puddle<br>cable<br>title<br>haggle<br>enable<br>bugle | treasure<br>feature<br>allure<br>measure<br>creature<br>manure | antique<br>character<br>phony<br>school<br>chef<br>gopher | vacation<br>delicious<br>social<br>permission<br>television<br>spatial | rhombus<br>autumn<br>numb<br>wrinkle<br>ghost<br>gnat |

To make reading and writing even more fun, have your child write a story using some of the words above. Or, encourage your child to come up with their own nonsense words using the spelling patterns.

Happy learning!

# Lesson 1 | Consonant Plus -*le*

*Review and Pretest*

## Introduce the New Concept

Take a moment to review the following syllabication rules covered in previous units. Today students will learn the last and final rule on this list! Ask your students to copy rule number 8 in their notebooks.

1. All syllables have one vowel sound.
2. Compound words should be divided between the two base words.
3. If two consonants appear in-between two vowels, divide them in half.
4. If three consonants appear between two vowels, determine which two belong together. Blends and digraphs should not be separated.
5. When one consonant is in between two vowels, first try dividing after the consonant to keep the vowel closed in. If that doesn't sound right, try dividing before the consonant to keep the vowel open.
6. Never divide a vowel team or diphthong in half.
7. If there are two vowels in the middle of a multisyllabic word that do not work as a team, divide them in half.
8. The syllable type consonant -*le* pattern is its own syllable and should be divided as one.

Now write down the following words. Notice that the words in the left column have open (long) vowels, and the words in the right column are closed in by the consonant.

| open | closed |
|------|--------|
| cable | puddle |
| title | gurgle |
| bugle | castle |

Teach your students to divide words immediately before the consonant -*le*. If the letter before that is a vowel, it is open. If it is a consonant, it is closed.

## Finger Tapping

| | | |
|------|--------|--------|
| cradle | 5 taps | c-r-a(pound) d-le(pound) |
| crumble | 6 taps | c-r-u-m(pound) b-le(pound) |

## Elkonin Boxes

| lit | tle |
|-----|-----|

## Concept-Picture Connection

Guide Word(s): castle, stable, puddle

## Multisensory Connections

| | | |
|---|---|---|
| tickle | ruffle | needle |
| hassle | title | whistle |

# Consonant Plus -*le*

**Read each word below.**

| | | |
|---|---|---|
| drizzle | noodle | castle |
| chuckle | ruffle | example |
| noble | sample | gentle |
| able | bubble | cradle |

**Read the sentences and circle the consonant plus -*le* words.**

1. Please pass me an apple to feed to the horse in the stable.

2. Look at the little duckling waddle across the road.

3. My uncle Tim will ride here on his bicycle.

4. Let's take turns carrying the paddles down to the creek.

5. The pop star is releasing her new hit single next week.

6. "That cradle will be perfect for the new baby!" Mona exclaimed.

7. The reporter wrote the article about the small castle that was discovered in the woods.

8. "Would you like a pickle sample?" the store clerk asked.

9. Grandma made her peanut brittle for the holiday party, but don't share the recipe because it's a big secret!

**Spell each word illustrated in the picture.**

b _____

c _____

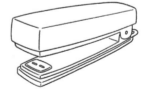

st _____

# Lesson 2 | Unaccented Syllables -*ure*, -*sure*, & -*ture*

## Review

## Introduce the New Concept

This lesson reviews the unaccented syllable patterns -*ure*, -*sure*, and -*ture*. As noted in the schwa lesson, an unaccented syllable is not said as clearly as an accented syllable. Encourage students to listen to the vowel sounds in the following words:

| -*ure* | -*sure* | -*ture* |
|--------|---------|---------|
| conjure | pleasure | mixture |
| failure | erasure | feature |
| obscure | fissure | suture |

In the -*sure* spelling pattern, we hear /zhur/, whereas in the *ture* pattern, we hear a clear /cher/. Note that words with the spellings -*cher* or -*tcher* are often professions or hobbies as in teacher and pitcher, while words with the -*ture* spelling are not. In all other words with a clear consonant and the /ure/ sound, students should spell with -*ure*.

## Finger Tapping

| | | |
|---|---|---|
| culture | 4 taps | c-u-l(pound) ture(pound) |
| treasure | 4 taps | t-r-ea(pound) sure(pound) |

## Elkonin Boxes

| lec | ture |
|-----|------|

## Concept-Picture Connection

Guide Word(s): measure, nature, injure

## Multisensory Connections

| | | |
|---|---|---|
| rancher | future | treasure |
| figure | posture | closure |

## Mini Assessment

Ask students to spell the following words: *texture*, *noble*, *figure*, and *candle*.

# Unaccented Syllables -*ure*, -*sure*, & -*ture*

**Read each word below.**

| | | |
|---|---|---|
| pasture | butcher | capture |
| injure | nature | leisure |
| catcher | marcher | departure |
| fissure | rapture | fracture |

**Read the sentences and circle the words containing -*ure*, -*sure*, and -*ture*.**

1. Legend has it that treasure is buried in the pasture at Rancher Joe's.

2. The catcher injured himself, so the baseball team will have a sub for the next few weeks.

3. My favorite thing about visiting other countries is that you get to learn about other cultures.

4. Suzanna and Piper will listen to the lecture at State University.

5. "I can assure you, that feature is one of our most popular," the salesman insisted.

6. "We are concerned about the moisture coming through the ceiling," the women said to the realtor while they were looking at homes for sale.

7. It is important that we dispose of our trash correctly, and not in nature.

8. The teacher felt great pleasure when she saw that all of her students earned high marks on the latest reading test.

9. Please sit on the bleachers while the teachers prepare the gym for the pep rally.

10. Have you seen the archers? They are needed to start the show.

Name: _____ Date: _____

# Consonant Plus -*le*, -*ure*, -*sure*, & -*ture* Mini Assessment

**Read the following words:**

| | | |
|---|---|---|
| cable | conjure | failure |
| structure | pimple | feature |
| hobble | stable | pleasure |

**Try your best to spell each word you hear.**

1. _____

2. _____

3. _____

4. _____

# Lesson 3 | Sounds of -que /k/, hard ch /k/, soft ch /sh/, & ph

*Review*

## Introduce the New Concept

Encourage students to listen to the sounds in the following words:

| -que | hard *ch* | soft *ch* | *ph* |
|------|-----------|-----------|------|
| unique | school | charade | phone |
| mosque | cholera | chef | gopher |

All of these patterns differ from previously introduced patterns. These patterns are not nearly as common as others that make the same sounds, but they occur often enough to be taught explicitly.

In the word antique, the -*que* makes a /k/ sound. In the word chef, we hear a /sh/ sound. Most words with these spelling sounds are derived from French words.

In the word school, the *ch* makes a /k/ sound. Most words with these sounds are derived from Greek words.

In the word phone, the *ph* forms a consonant digraph to make a new sound, /f/. These words are typically derived from Greek.

## Finger Tapping

| chaos | 4 taps | ch-a(pound) o-s(pound) |
|-------|--------|------------------------|
| opaque | 4 taps | o(pound) p-a-que(pound) |

## Elkonin Boxes

| el | e | phant |
|----|---|-------|

## Concept-Picture Connection

Guide Word(s): antique, school, chef, phone

## Multisensory Connections

| critique | chrome | antique |
|----------|--------|---------|
| chaperone | alphabet | pistachio |

# Sounds of -*que*, *ch*, & *ph*

**Read each word below.**

| | | |
|---|---|---|
| sphere | Michigan | chiffon |
| machine | bisque | paragraph |
| clique | photogenic | chord |
| cholesterol | mystique | archive |
| chiropractor | anchor | chute |

**Try your best to read these sentences.**

1. My stomach is so full after that huge bowl of seafood bisque!

2. "Where are the chaperones for the Lake Michigan trip?" the teacher wondered aloud as she looked at the empty hallway.

3. My mother is an expert at growing orchids, but I have no skills in gardening.

4. Buster and Jack came down with a nasty case of bronchitis, so we will need to attend the elephant sanctuary without them.

5. The motorcycle's chrome gleamed in the sunlight as it zoomed down the road.

6. "I am going to the boutique to search for a dress for tonight's photo shoot. Would you like to come?" my mother asked expectantly.

7. The pistachio ice cream has a unique but well-loved flavor.

8. Masha and Chloe will bring quiche to brunch on Sunday.

9. The schooner dropped anchor just outside of the dock.

# Lesson 4 | Sounds of *ti*, *si*, & *ci*

*Review*

## Introduce the New Concept

Today's lesson focuses on the sounds of *ti*, *si*, and *ci*, which typically occur in *tion*, *sion*, and *cious* endings. These patterns often occur at the end of words and make either a /sh/ or a /zsh/ sound. The pattern *sion* can sound like a soft /sh/ or a /zsh/. The pattern *cious* has a /sh/ sound for the *ci*, while /ous/ sounds like us. Encourage students to listen to the sounds in the following words:

| *ti* | *si* | *ci* |
|---|---|---|
| vacation | profession | delicious |
| caption | television | gracious |

These patterns are typically associated with Latin. Knowing common Latin meanings can be very helpful when determining the meaning of unknown words. The endings *ion*, *tion*, and *sion* all mean the act of, state of, or result of something. The suffix *cious* or *ious* means full of having something.

There are a few other patterns that make a /sh/ sound at the end of words, but they are rare. You may choose to include them in your instruction to advanced students. Here are a few examples:

| *ce* | *xi* | *sci* |
|---|---|---|
| ocean | anxious | luscious |
| crustacean | obnoxious | conscious |
| licorice | flexion | |
| herbaceous | complexion | |

## Finger Tapping

| tension | 4 taps | t-e-n(pound) sion(pound) |
|---|---|---|
| notion | 3 taps | n-o(pound) tion(pound) |

## Elkonin Boxes

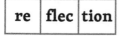

| re | flec | tion |
|---|---|---|

## Concept-Picture Connection

Guide Word(s): vacation, profession, television, delicious

## Multisensory Connections

| | | |
|---|---|---|
| starvation | gracious | dimension |
| quotation | session | reflection |

## Mini Assessment

Ask students to spell the following words: *chiffon, initial, phonograph,* and *vacation.*

# Sounds of *ti*, *si*, & -*ci*

**Read each word below.**

| | | |
|---|---|---|
| section | location | delicious |
| direction | acacia | prediction |
| function | emotion | suction |
| repulsion | injection | possession |
| comprehension | expansion | invention |

**Try your best to read the sentences.**

1. The construction workers are going to start pouring the foundation today.

2. Hank is going to school to study ancient Egyptian history.

3. "Please pay for park admission at the concession stand on the right side," the speaker blared as the family approached the amusement park.

4. With permission slip in hand, the middle schoolers pranced to the door of the school, excited to go on the trip to the nature preserve.

5. Most toddlers lack patience," the mother muttered as she shook her head at the whining two-year-old.

6. It is important to take special caution when you approach a construction site. The floor may not be stable.

7. On the mission to the moon, Neil Armstrong, Michael Collins, and Buzz Aldrin had to go through many special precautions to stay safe.

8. Although I prefer fiction, I also enjoy nonfiction texts.

9. There are many precious artifacts in the Biltmore mansion in North Carolina.

10. "Have you considered trying a martial arts class?" Ben mentioned to Dina.

# Mini Assessment - *que*, *ch*, *ph*, *ti*, *si*, & *ci*

**Read the following words:**

| | | |
|---|---|---|
| photogenic | mystique | temptation |
| pension | social | anchor |
| expression | quiche | gracious |

**Try your best to spell each word you hear.**

1. _____

2. _____

3. _____

4. _____

# Lesson 5 | Silent Letter Pairs

*Review*

## Introduce the New Concept

Congratulations on making it to the final lesson! While this book does not cover every possible spelling pattern, it covers all of the common patterns. It will give your students an excellent foundation for decoding and encoding unfamiliar words!

To date, we covered several common silent letters such as *wh* and *igh*. This lesson is devoted to the less common silent letter pairs. Encourage students to view the following list of words:

**silent letter pairs**

| | |
|---|---|
| rhyme | knight |
| ghost | gnaw |
| lamb | wren |
| autumn | |

By this point your students can probably read many of these simply by being exposed to these words in text. Go through each word, and have your students identify the silent letter.

## Finger Tapping

| | | |
|---|---|---|
| climb | 4 taps | c-l-i-mb |
| gnash | 3 taps | gn-a-sh |

## Elkonin Boxes

| wrist | band |
|---|---|

## Concept-Picture Connection

Guide Word(s): rhino, ghost, lamb, autumn, knight, gnome, wren

## Multisensory Connections

| | | |
|---|---|---|
| thumb | knot | know |
| rhubarb | rhythm | sovereign |

# Silent Letter Pairs

**Read each word below.**

| | | |
|---|---|---|
| assign | design | write |
| rhyme | afghan | gnome |
| condemn | reign | spaghetti |
| knight | wrinkle | knot |

**Try your best to read these sentences.**

1. I learned how to knead dough for rhubarb pie when I visited my grandma this summer.

2. We went to the "Ghosts and Ghouls" party at the restaurant last year and it was a lot of fun!

3. There are many species of rhino that are endangered.

4. "Please place your writing materials in your knapsacks before moving on to the next activity," the teacher requested.

5. To prepare for the snow, I put on my knit hat and my warmest jacket.

6. Wren and her father wrapped presents for the children at the shelter.

7. The mouse feigned ignorance when the crumb dropped on the floor, but he ran to it as soon as the coast was clear!

8. The crisp autumn air rustled through the colorful leaves.

9. "Try not to make much noise with your wrappers while I am speaking," the expert requested of the children as he prepared the demonstration.

**Read the words below. For the silent pairs, underline the silent letter and circle the letter that makes the sound.**

| | | |
|---|---|---|
| rhombus | sign | written |
| dinghy | | lamb |

# Unit 9 Review: Decodable Story

**Read the following story and then answer the questions.**

The day had finally arrived! Autumn and her uncle, Noah, were on a plane headed to Ireland to photograph the castles and other nature scenes. Uncle Noah was the head travel photographer for a major publication in New York City. Autumn was a new photographer, but was hoping to learn some tips from a professional like her uncle.

Finally, their plane landed at Dublin Airport. Noah and Autumn got into a taxi. Autumn looked around in wonder. The gentle hills rolled around her in a sea of emerald. They headed to Charleville Castle, a location that was known for its historic Druid roots. Legend also had it that ghosts roamed the castle corridors at night.

As the city thinned out and nature began to show itself, Noah shot photographs out the window. He showed Autumn how to use the light to capture the best shot, and explained how different lenses would work to filter the shot. He handed his camera to Autumn to let her try a few shots. Then she started applying the same settings to her own camera. She started to get into a rhythm and actually got a few decent shots!

They pulled up to the castle just as the sun started to sink down to the horizon. Autumn's initial thought was that it looked majestic, but also a bit spooky. The stone walls stood strong with very few signs of crumbling or deterioration. The architecture was amazingly intact after hundreds of years in the elements.

Noah and Autumn circled the stone structure as they both took shots. Suddenly, Autumn noticed something eerie in one of the windows. Something opaque seemed to block the light in one area. "Look," she hollered to her uncle, but by that time, the figure was gone. Autumn chalked it up to her being tired and didn't think about it again.

The rest of their trip went by and they both got dozens of "perfect" shots. Autumn improved her technique substantially, and Noah even chose one of her shots for the travel piece in his magazine.

As they sat at the table reviewing all of the photos for selection, Autumn came upon one of her shots from the Charleville Castle. As she peered closely at the picture, she saw that opaque figure again. Her uncle noticed the figure too! However, in the light of the daytime sun, she saw what the figure really was—a cat! While seeing a ghost would have been pretty cool, Autumn and her uncle were both secretly glad that it had only been a cat!

**1.** Where did Autumn go? Why?

_____

_____

_____

_____

**2.** What did she see there?

_____

_____

_____

_____

**3.** Where do you want to travel? What do you want to see while you're there?

_____

_____

_____

_____

# Unit 9 Post-Test

**Read the following words:**

| | | |
|---|---|---|
| gaggle | opaque | staple |
| bugle | photograph | rhythm |
| creature | invention | crumb |
| endure | transmission | ghastly |
| erasure | division | known |
| charade | spacious | gnash |
| charisma | quiche | writ |

**Try your best to read these sentences.**

1. "You sure have a knack for building things, Hannah," her friend Noah said with admiration.

2. Did you assign the foundation plans to the machine operator?

3. The chef said the butcher got the meat from the local pasture, so it should be delicious.

4. The Halloween decorations look great! I especially love the ghouls and ghosts!

5. The photographer was able to capture great shots of us on vacation.

**Read the words below. For the silent pairs, underline the silent letter and circle the letter that makes the sound.**

rhyme            feign            wren

ghoulish                    limb

# Appendix

## Initial Assessment

To help you determine each student's current reading and spelling levels at the beginning of the school year, we recommend you administer a couple of assessments. Consider readministering these tests at the middle and end of the year to gauge progress.

### Reading Assessment

To administer the reading assessment, begin by asking your students to read orally the list of words on the Student Reading Sheet on page 283. Tell students to start from number one and proceed down the list while you mark words read incorrectly on the Assessment Teacher Tracking Sheet on page 281. When a student makes two or more errors in a reading section, end the assessment and proceed to the spelling portion of the test.

### Spelling Assessment

Give each student the Student Spelling Sheet on page 285. Start from Unit 1 regardless of your student's age or grade. Read off the words in the spelling portion of the Assessment Teacher Tracking Sheet on page 281 and ask your students to spell each word on their Student Spelling Sheet. Review each individual sheet and then mark off any words spelled incorrectly on your Assessment Teacher Tracking Sheet. End the test when your student gets two or more spelling errors in a section.

Students who do not know their consonant and short vowel sounds should begin in Unit 1.

### Where to Start

We suggest starting in the unit in which your student gets two or more reading or spelling errors. For sections in which your student only gets one error, you may choose to begin with the individual lesson(s) that correlate with the missed skill.

# Assessment Teacher Tracking Sheet

Directions: Highlight any words your students miss.

| Unit 1 | Unit 2 | Unit 3 | Unit 4 | Unit 5 |
|---|---|---|---|---|
| **Reading** | **Reading** | **Reading** | **Reading** | **Reading** |
| big | sham | catnap | fade | stay |
| fed | plan | sunset | close | rescue |
| chap | squint | pumpkin | twine | pail |
| sack | strict | hundred | theme | coach |
| dolls | small | racket | plume | fruit |
| wish | shrimp | wagon | homemade | reach |
| thin | swing | scold | biting | greed |
| foxes | honk | find | valentine | toe |
| fuss | match | hopping | give | peach |
| duck | plank | mild | expensive | grail |
| | | | | |
| Correct _____ /10 | Correct _____ /10 | Correct _____ /10 | Correct _____ /10 | Correct _____ /10 |
| **Spelling** | **Spelling** | **Spelling** | **Spelling** | **Spelling** |
| fit | ham | bathtub | lake | boat |
| deck | ball | tunnel | tone | clay |
| chin | twist | bolt | spine | steam |
| shops | rung | cabin | sunshine | fruit |
| buzz | sang | dripping | olive | pie |
| | | | | |
| Correct _____ /5 | Correct _____ /5 | Correct _____ /5 | Correct _____ /5 | Correct _____ /5 |

| Unit 6 | Unit 7 | Unit 8 | Unit 9 |
|--------|--------|--------|--------|
| **Reading** | **Reading** | **Reading** | **Reading** |
| shy | later | taut | giggle |
| baby | burning | spoiled | stable |
| relax | skirt | crouched | conjure |
| Alaska | barn | cooler | moisture |
| locate | ledge | hook | chaos |
| moment | dreary | steak | technique |
| client | scurry | dreadful | terminate |
| families | burden | weigh | measure |
| planted | center | flightless | ghost |
| tripped | gist | donkey | phase |
| | | | |
| Correct _____ /10 | Correct _____ /10 | Correct _____ /10 | Correct _____ /10 |
| **Spelling** | **Spelling** | **Spelling** | **Spelling** |
| unit | weary | bookworm | hurdle |
| cleaned | scarf | enjoy | monarch |
| latest | worn | brighter | puncture |
| poet | hurry | chewing | chaperone |
| apex | germs | vein | triumph |
| | | | |
| Correct _____ /5 | Correct _____ /5 | Correct _____ /5 | Correct _____ /5 |

# Student Reading Sheet

| Unit 1 | Unit 2 | Unit 3 | Unit 4 | Unit 5 |
| --- | --- | --- | --- | --- |
| big | sham | catnap | fade | stay |
| fed | plan | sunset | close | rescue |
| chap | squint | pumpkin | twine | pail |
| sack | strict | hundred | theme | coach |
| dolls | small | racket | plume | fruit |
| wish | shrimp | wagon | homemade | reach |
| thin | swing | scold | biting | greed |
| foxes | honk | find | valentine | toe |
| fuss | match | hopping | give | peach |
| duck | plank | mild | expensive | grail |

| Unit 6 | Unit 7 | Unit 8 | Unit 9 |
|--------|--------|--------|--------|
| shy | later | taut | giggle |
| baby | burning | spoiled | stable |
| relax | skirt | crouched | conjure |
| Alaska | barn | cooler | moisture |
| locate | ledge | hook | chaos |
| moment | dreary | steak | technique |
| client | scurry | dreadful | terminate |
| families | burden | weigh | measure |
| planted | center | flightless | ghost |
| tripped | gist | donkey | phase |

# Student Spelling Sheet

Name: _____ Date: _____

**Unit:** _____

1. _____

2. _____

3. _____

4. _____

5. _____

**Unit:** _____

1. _____

2. _____

3. _____

4. _____

5. _____

**Unit:** _____

1. _____

2. _____

3. _____

4. _____

5. _____

**Unit:** _____

1. _____

2. _____

3. _____

4. _____

5. _____

# Guide Words List

**Unit 1**
1. pig, bat
2. tree, dinosaur
3. kit, grapes
4. igloo
5. flower, van
6. elephant
7. sun, zipper
8. alligator
9. cheese, jam
10. monster, nest
11. olive
12. wing, hive, whisper
13. list, railroad
14. umbrella
15. Spelling Rule *c, k, -ck*: cat, kit, duck
16. fox, xylophone, exist
17. yak
18. question
19. thunder, there
20. shell, measure
21. The Doubling Rule *ss, ll, ff, z*: kiss
22. Plural Spelling Rule *-s, -es, -lves*: frogs, halves, wishes

**Unit 2**
1. crab
2. splash, shrub
3. mask
4. Spelling Rule *-ct* Ending: collect
5. Spelling Rule *ch/-tch*: beach, lunch, catch
6. pan, jam
7. ball

8. king, gong, lung, bang
9. rink, honk, bunk, sank

**Unit 3**
1. shellfish
2. cactus, rabbit, pumpkin, anthem
3. lemon, rocket
4. Closed Syllable Exceptions: child, find, mold, colt, host
5. The 1•1•1 Spelling Rule: hop-hopping

**Unit 4**
1. cake
2. kite, cone
3. here, cube, tune
4. reptile, pinecone, valentine
5. Spelling Rule *-ive* Exception: live, live
6. Spelling Rule *e*-Drop Rule: bite-biting, tasted

**Unit 5**
1. beach, tree
2. snail, play
3. boat, toe
4. rescue, clue, fruit, pie

**Unit 6**
1. cry, she
2. baby, relax
3. lion, poem
4. animal, Alaska
5. Spelling Rule Plurals Ending in *y*: families, decays
6. Spelling Rule Suffix *-ed*: cleaned, planted, jumped

**Unit 7**
1. fern, bird, hurt
2. barn, scare, dollar, wart
3. corn, world, doctor, core
4. year, pearl, bear
5. flurry, carry, ferret
6. Spelling Rule Soft *c* and *g*: city, gem
7. Spelling Rule *-ge* and *-dge*: huge, fudge

**Unit 8**
1. draw, astronaut
2. boy, coil
3. owl, snow, ouch
4. pool, book
5. break, head
6. feud, chew
7. night, monkey, sleigh
8. Spelling Rule *ie/ei*: cookie, receive

**Unit 9**
1. castle, stable, puddle
2. measure, nature, injure
3. antique, school, chef, phone
4. vacation, profession, delicious, television
5. rhino, ghost, lamb, autumn, knight, gnome, wren

# Spelling Rules Chart

This chart covers 16 of the most common spelling rules that are taught explicitly in this book.

| Pattern | Rule | Examples | Exceptions |
|---|---|---|---|
| *c/k* | Hard *c* is used before consonants and the vowels *a*, *o*, and *u*. *K* is used before *e* and *i*. | cat<br>cob<br>cuff<br>kit<br>kept | koala<br>kangaroo<br>Korea<br>skate<br>Kung Fu |
| *k/-ck/-c* | A -*ck* is used at the end of a one-syllable word right after a short vowel. Use *k* in all other instances. | lick<br>deck<br>bake<br>steak<br>milk | Two Syllables:<br>attack<br>hammock<br>When a suffix begins with *e*, *i*, or *y*, add a *k* after the *c*. |
| | A -*c* usually goes at the end of two-syllable words ending in the /k/ sound. | mimic<br>panic | mimicked<br>panicking |
| **The Doubling Rule** (*ff, ss, ll, zz*) | If a word ends with a short vowel followed by *f*, *l*, *s*, *or z*, double it! | toss<br>huff<br>will<br>jazz | gross<br>bus<br>chef<br>gal |
| **Plural Spelling Rule** -*s*, -*es*, -*lves* | To make a word plural that ends in *s*, *x*, *z*, *ch*, *sh*, or a consonant plus *o*, you must add -*es*. | run-runs<br>kit-kits | hero-heroes<br>potato-potatoes<br>tomato-tomatoes |
| | For words ending in *f*, change it to *v* and add -*es*. For all other letter endings, add -*s*. | half-halves<br>calf-calves | This rule does not apply to irregular nouns:<br>mouse-mice<br>tooth-teeth<br>foot-feet<br>man-men |
| | When a word ends in *s*, the *s* may sound like /s/ or /z/. | kiss-kisses<br>box-boxes | Some words don't change at all:<br>fish-fish<br>sheep-sheep<br>deer-deer |
| **-*ct* Rule** | For words that end with the /kt/ sound, use the spelling -*ct*. | collect<br>act<br>project | |

| Pattern | Rule | Examples | Exceptions |
|---|---|---|---|
| **-ch/-tch** | If a word ends in the /ch/ sound, use -*tch* if it follows a short vowel. Use -*ch* if it comes after a long vowel or consonant. | mulch<br>stitch<br>bunch<br>notch<br>teach | much<br>such<br>rich<br>attach |
| **Closed Syllable Exceptions** | If a word has the pattern -*old*, -*ost*, -*olt*, -*ind*, or -*ild*, the vowel is long. | kind<br>wild<br>bold<br>post<br>colt | -*ost* and -*ind* can be short or long as in:<br>cost<br>lost<br>wind |
| **1•1•1 Rule** | If a word ends in one vowel followed by one consonant, you must double the consonant when adding a vowel suffix such as in -*ing*, -*ed*, and -*est*. | hop-hopping<br>flip-flipped<br>sad-saddest<br>wet-wetter | Don't double the consonant in words ending with -*w*, -*x*, or -*y*, as in:<br>taxed<br>flowing<br>staying |
| **-ive Exception** | When a word ends in -*ive*, the vowel can be short or long. | give<br>five<br>strive<br>live (both) | |
| **e-Drop Rule** | When a word ends in silent *e*, drop the *e* before adding a vowel suffix such as -*ing*, -*ed*, -*er*, or -*est*.<br><br>Keep it if the suffix begins with a consonant such as -*ly*, -*ment*, or -*ty*. | lone-lonely<br>chose-chosen<br>hole-holes<br>taste-tasted<br>use-useless<br>hype-hyped<br>hope-hoping | The *e* is not dropped in words ending with -*ee*, -*oe*, or -*ye* as in:<br>seeing<br>hoeing<br>dyeing<br><br>Other exceptions:<br>acreage<br>mileage<br>singeing |
| **Plurals Ending in y** | If a word ends in a vowel sound and then *y*, just add -*s*. If a word ends in a consonant and then *y*, drop the *y* and add -*ies*. | baby-babies<br>monkey-monkeys<br>lady-ladies<br>play-plays | This rule does not apply to proper nouns. |

| Pattern | Rule | Examples | Exceptions |
|---|---|---|---|
| **Suffix -ed Rule** | Suffix -ed can make 3 sounds: /d/ (moved), /ed/ (planted), and /t/ (jumped) | | |
| | Base words that end with a t or d sound like /ed/ at the end. | jumped<br>ducked<br>hatched | |
| | Base words that end with a voiceless sound such as p, k, s, f, ch, soft th, and sh sound like /t/. | begged<br>bathed<br>stayed | |
| | Base words that end with a voiced sound such as b, g, v, j, z, l, m, n, r, hard th, or long vowel sound like a /d/. | molded<br>posted | |
| **-rr Exception** | When there are two r's next to each other in a word, the vowel often keeps its own sound. | carrot<br>scurry<br>horrid | The pattern -err sounds like /ār/<br>errand<br>terry |
| **Soft c and g** | If c or g is followed by the vowels e, i, or y, the letter is soft, as in city and giant. | city<br>giraffe<br>cycle<br>gyrate<br>center | gear<br>get<br>girl<br>tiger<br>gift |
| **-ge/-dge** | Use -dge after a short vowel. Use -ge after a long vowel. | fudge<br>pledge<br>wage<br>page<br>purge<br>strange | |
| **ei/ie** | I before e except after c or in words that sound like /ay/. | believe<br>grief<br>thief<br>achieve<br>friend<br>receipt | caffeine<br>species<br>height<br>ancient |

# Sight Words List
## The First 100 Words

### Unit 1

| | | | | | |
|---|---|---|---|---|---|
| and | do | is | when | this | may |
| the | we | day | which | it | then |
| be | by | my | had | have | than |
| look | a | to | like | not | out |
| said | no | she | will | on | more |
| you | at | he | see | make | |
| can | but | was | them | down | |
| go | get | one | in | how | |
| I | all | two | first | or | |
| so | of | did | come | with | |

### Unit 2

| | | | | |
|---|---|---|---|---|
| what | as | for | are | has |
| up | her | if | use | sit |
| from | an | your | him | been |
| who | his | that | there | many |

### Unit 3

| | | | | |
|---|---|---|---|---|
| each | find | long | they | about |
| made | now | way | time | oil |
| were | some | part | would | these |

### Unit 4

| | | | | |
|---|---|---|---|---|
| could | call | word | their | number |
| into | other | write | water | people |

# The Second 100 Words

## Unit 4 (continued)

| | | | |
|---|---|---|---|
| over | sound | only | work |
| new | take | little | know |

## Unit 5

| | | | | |
|---|---|---|---|---|
| place | back | after | name | think |
| year | give | things | good | say |
| live | most | our | sentence | great |
| me | very | just | man | where |

## Unit 6

| | | | | | |
|---|---|---|---|---|---|
| help | before | too | any | boy | want |
| through | line | means | same | follow | |
| much | right | old | tell | came | |

## Unit 7

| | | | | | |
|---|---|---|---|---|---|
| show | form | set | does | large | even |
| also | three | put | another | must | such |
| around | small | end | well | big | because |

## Unit 8

| | | | | | |
|---|---|---|---|---|---|
| turn | went | land | move | picture | play |
| here | men | different | try | again | spell |
| why | read | home | kind | change | |
| ask | need | us | hand | off | |

## Unit 9

| | | | | | |
|---|---|---|---|---|---|
| air | house | letter | found | learn | world |
| away | point | mother | study | should | |
| animal | page | answer | still | America | |

# ABOUT THE AUTHORS

**Heather MacLeod-Vidal** graduated from the University of Tampa with a degree in elementary education. She then worked for four years as a classroom teacher in 3rd and 5th grades. After attending Orton-Gillingham training in 2014, Heather began Treetops Educational Interventions, a company that specializes in assisting students with learning differences. She began tutoring students after school using the Orton-Gillingham method and saw huge growth in students who were not making progress using traditional classroom methods. Soon after, Heather left the classroom to work full-time with students who have learning differences. She expanded her business to include tutors with different specialties (including coauthor Kristina Smith). After several years of tutoring and attending a variety of reading and Orton-Gillingham trainings, Heather and Kristina set out to create their own curriculum using the methods they had learned, implemented, and improved over the years. Since their launch on Teachers Pay Teachers in 2017, Heather and Kristina have listed and sold hundreds of products using the Orton-Gillingham method and other reading subjects. In 2019 and 2020, they were also honored as Milestone sellers on Teachers Pay Teachers. Heather currently works with students who have dyslexia and other learning differences at a Tampa Bay area school. She lives in St. Petersburg, Florida, with her husband, two children, and a variety of rescue animals.

**Kristina Smith** received a bachelor of arts degree in sociology from the University of South Florida. Upon graduating, she began her teaching career with Hillsborough County Public Schools, where she taught pre-kindergarten to 5th grade students with various learning disabilities. Continuing to pursue her love of helping children, she attended Florida State University where she received her master of social work degree. For two years, Kristina provided therapy to children with emotional and mental health disorders before she narrowed her focus back to children with learning difficulties. Since 2014, she has trained in Orton-Gillingham, taught numerous students who struggle with reading and math, and has coauthored a curriculum for teachers who wish to help their struggling students with reading. Kristina is still an educator and resides in Panama City Beach, Florida, with her husband.

To learn more about Heather and Kristina's resources for struggling readers, please visit their website, treetopseducation.com, or search Treetops Educational Interventions on Teachers Pay Teachers.

Printed in the USA
CPSIA information can be obtained
at www.ICGtesting.com
CBHW080334290524
9227CB00007B/22